Series/Number 07-158

INTRODUCTION TO THE COMPARATIVE METHOD WITH BOOLEAN ALGEBRA

Daniele Caramani

University of St. Gallen, Switzerland

SAGE

Los Angeles ■ London ■ New Delhi ■ Singapore

For information:

SAGE Publications, Inc.
2455 Teller Road
Thousand Oaks, California 91320
E-mail: order@sagepub.com

SAGE Publications Ltd.
1 Oliver's Yard
55 City Road
London EC1Y 1SP
United Kingdom

SAGE Publications India Pvt. Ltd.
B 1/I 1 Mohan Cooperative
  Industrial Area
Mathura Road, New Delhi 110 044
India

SAGE Publications Asia-Pacific
  Pte. Ltd.
33 Pekin Street #02-01
Far East Square
Singapore 048763

Printed in the United States of America

Library of Congress Cataloging-in-Publication Data

Caramani, Daniele.
Introduction to the comparative method with Boolean algebra/Daniele Caramani.
    p. cm. — (Quantitative applications in the social sciences; 158)
Includes bibliographical references and index.
ISBN 978-1-4129-0975-4 (pbk.)
    1. Social sciences—Comparative method. 2. Algebra, Boolean. I. Title.

H61.C2465 2009
300.1′511324—dc22   2008011025

This book is printed on acid-free paper.

08   09   10   11   12   10 9 8   7   6   5   4   3   2   1

Acquisitions Editors:	Vicki Knight, Lisa Cuevas Shaw
Associate Editor:	Sean Connelly
Editorial Assistant:	Lauren Habib
Production Editor:	Cassandra Margaret Seibel
Copy Editor:	QuADS Prepress (P) Ltd.
Typesetter:	C&M Digitals (P) Ltd.
Proofreader:	Charlotte Waisner
Indexer:	Jean Casalegno
Cover Designer:	Candice Harman
Marketing Manager:	Stephanie Adams

CONTENTS

ABOUT THE AUTHOR

Daniele Caramani is Professor of Comparative Politics and Methods at the University of St. Gallen, Switzerland. He is the author of the book and CD-ROM *Elections in Western Europe Since 1815* (2000) and *The Nationalization of Politics* (2004), for which he received the "Stein Rokkan Prize for Comparative Research in the Social Sciences." He has also edited *Comparative Politics* (2008). His current research focuses on the integration of European electorates and party systems. His paper titled "Is There a European Electorate and What Does It Look Like? Evidence from Electoral Volatility Measures, 1976–2004" has appeared in *West European Politics* (Vol. 29, No. 1, 2006) and has been awarded the "Vincent Wright Memorial Prize" for the best article in 2006.

PREFACE AND ACKNOWLEDGMENTS

This book provides the reader with a concise introduction to comparison in the social sciences. It shows that comparison is a basic principle in all types of empirical inquiry—both the large-scale comparative designs that rely on statistical techniques and the "comparative method" that since the 1970s has been high on the social sciences' agenda (Holt & Turner, 1970; Lijphart, 1971; Przeworski & Teune, 1970; Sartori, 1970; Smelser, 1973) and that more recently has been reinvigorated through Ragin's and others' work (Brady & Collier, 2004; Ragin, 1987, 2000).

Principles of comparison are dealt with by introducing their *logical* foundations: classification, Mill's methods of inductive inference, necessary and sufficient conditions, and Boolean algebra. This follows the well-known suggestion that "political scientists turn to [the] rules of logic" to increase the deductive power of their theories (Holt & Richardson, 1970, p. 70), but also provides the tools to understand current advances, namely in the fields of "qualitative comparative analysis," "small-N" approaches, and "fuzzy-set" methods.

The book is conceived as an introductory text that does not require particular methodological, statistical, or logical training. Principles and procedures are explained making only indispensable reference to logical operators. As the book has also been written with an eye to its use as a textbook, it separates unsettled questions from shared standards in methodological debates. Furthermore, guidelines for comparative research presented here distinguish phases of empirical research for which "objective" rules exist, from phases in which "subjective" decisions by the researcher are involved.

For comments I wish to thank Klaus Armingeon, Dirk Berg-Schlosser, Ingrid van Biezen, Bear Braumoeller, Bernhard Ebbinghaus, Gary King, Hanspeter Kriesi, B. Guy Peters, Charles Ragin, Benoît Rihoux, Carsten Schneider, and the late Charles Tilly, as well as Sage's anonymous referees. I have also greatly profited from undergraduate and graduate teaching experiences in various universities. All mistakes remain nonetheless entirely mine.

D.C.

SYMBOLS

$=$	Equal to.
$\neq$	Different from.
$<$	Less than.
$>$	More than.
$\leq$	Equal to or less than.
$\geq$	Equal to or more than.
$\equiv$	Equivalence or double conditional (also symbolized as $\leftrightarrow$).
$\sim$	Negation, "nonoccurrence;" replaces the verbal symbols NOT.
$\cdot$	Conjunction, intersection or Boolean multiplication; the midlevel dot replaces the verbal symbols AND (also symbolized as $\wedge$).
$\vee$	Disjunction or Boolean addition; the "wedge" or "vee" replaces the verbal symbols OR (also symbolized as $+$).
$\supset$	Implication; the "horseshoe" replaces the verbal symbols IF . . . , THEN . . . (also symbolized as $\rightarrow$).
$\therefore$	Conclusion of syllogism; the triangular dots replace the verbal symbols THEREFORE.
C	Cause or antecedent (also symbolized as p).
E	Effect or consequent (also symbolized as q).
H	Hypothesis.

ABBREVIATIONS

MDSD	Most Different Systems Design.
MD-SO	Most Different With Similar Outcome.
MS-DO	Most Similar With Different Outcome.
MSSD	Most Similar Systems Design.
QCA	Qualitative Comparative Analysis.

EDITORIAL NOTE

The bibliography includes methodological work only. Examples of comparative analysis are drawn from published work. However, to have as much as possible a homogeneous methodological bibliography, references to substantive research have been omitted.

INTRODUCTION TO THE COMPARATIVE METHOD WITH BOOLEAN ALGEBRA

Daniele Caramani
University of St. Gallen, Switzerland

> *"Il n'y a rien que l'esprit humain fasse si
> souvent que des comparaisons."*
>
> —*Encyclopédie*, Volume Three (1753).

CHAPTER 1. DEFINITION

Comparison is a fundamental principle of science as well as a basic element of everyday life. It is a spontaneous mental process, so that "[t]hinking without comparison is unthinkable" (Swanson, 1971, p. 145). Daily we compare lines in shops (shorter or longer), the weather from one day to the next (better or worse), the size of clothing articles (larger or smaller), the arrival of trains (earlier or later). Simple terms like "densely populated" make implicit comparisons (Smelser, 1976, p. 3). In the social sciences, researchers compare the quality of life between cities, the stability of governments across countries, economic behavior between social groups, and the impact of rituals on social cohesion. With classification (Bailey, 1994, in this same series), comparison is one of the crucial conceptual processes making the world intelligible.

Objects, Attributes, Values

In its simplest form, comparison can be defined as the juxtaposition of *values* (units of variation) of *attributes* (properties) shared by two or more *objects* or cases (units of observation). For example, according to the World Bank, the 2002 annual gross domestic product (GDP) growth (attribute) was 2.4% and 8.0% (values) in the United States and China (objects). Or the timing of democratization (attribute) has been precocious (value)

1

in Britain (object) and delayed in Russia. The same applies if we compare objects over time. Electoral volatility in Italy was 23.0 and 8.3 in 1948 and 1983, respectively. Here, the objects of the comparison are elections. That is to say that comparison is about variation: *variation in the score or value of a variable across a number of cases.*

In the first place, to compare means to describe variables. Together with explanation and prediction, description is one of the main tasks of scientific enterprise. Descriptive comparisons focus on the *degree of similarity* and *difference* between two or more cases. Descriptive comparisons can be (1) *nominal*—presence/absence or different types of attributes (e.g., the electoral system in Switzerland is proportional representation whereas in Britain it is plurality); (2) *ordinal*—more/less; or earlier/later and faster/slower in temporal comparisons (e.g., state formation occurred earlier in Britain than in Switzerland); or (3) *quantitative* (interval and ratio) when the values are continuous and quantifiable (e.g., the number of effective parties in Switzerland is 2.92 higher than in Britain).

Comparison as a Method

The intrinsic character of descriptive comparisons in all human activities leads to a first question. If comparison is a ubiquitous mental process, from daily life to scientific research, why do we speak of a comparative "method"? The answer is that the comparative *method* is something else—and more—than simply a natural mental activity. It is a method to analyze *relationships* between phenomena and their *causal connections*, that is, to test against empirical evidence alternative hypotheses on cause–effect relationships in the form of "if . . . , then . . . " statements. In addition to being an indispensable cognitive and descriptive tool, the comparative method is explanatory, a *method to control variation* (Smelser, 1976, p. 152) and to establish generalizations or "laws" between variables (Lijphart, 1971, p. 683; Sartori, 1970, p. 1035)—ultimately a *method of inductive inference.*

To compare, therefore, does not only mean to describe variation. Variation is necessary for *explanation.* Without variation (different scores or values of variables across cases), explanation is not possible. This is true for all types of comparisons, whether they are large-scale comparative studies based on a large number of cases analyzed through statistical (quantitative) techniques or small-scale comparative studies based on few cases analyzed through logical and Boolean algebra. Even though the label "comparative method" is today increasingly equated with this second approach, the fundamental principles are the same. In fact, most practitioners of the comparative method would agree that there are basic commonalities between "quantitative" and "qualitative" techniques.[1]

Accordingly, the comparative method can be defined as *a set of logically based procedures for systematically testing against empirical evidence alternative (or competing) hypotheses about causal connections between phenomena, and thereby either corroborate or reject them.* The comparative method aims at identifying lawlike "causal regularities" (Skocpol, 1984a, pp. 374–386). This analytical approach is not the only way of conducting comparative research (Peters, 1998, pp. 9–11). Comparativists also use other approaches, which, however, cannot be considered control methods—such as causal interpretations—because they do not test against empirical evidence hypotheses about causal connections (Skocpol, 1984a, p. 372).

Comparison and Other Methods

It is important to note that such a definition of the comparative method encompasses a number of other methods too. It does apply equally to experimental and statistical methods. It is not confined to what in recent years has come to be identified with a narrow definition of the comparative method—namely, comparison based on Mill's methods and Boolean algebra.

This leads to a second question. If the comparative method shares its analytical character with other methods—and the term "comparison" has indeed been applied to experimental and statistical methods by Durkheim and Parsons—*is there a difference between the comparative method and other methods*? What is specific about the comparative method?

Some authors maintain that without comparison all scientific thought is unimaginable (Swanson, 1971, p. 145) and that research, in one form or other, is unavoidably comparative (Lasswell, 1968, p. 3; Lieberson, 1985, p. 44). Almond notes (1966), "[i]t makes no sense to speak of a comparative method in political science since if it is a science, it goes without saying that it is comparative" (pp. 877–878). Because comparison constitutes the core of all scientific explanation (Armer, 1973; Bailey, 1982; Blalock, 1961; Nagel, 1961), some authors object to the logical and epistemological distinctiveness of the comparative method (Grimshaw, 1973, p. 18). As Klingman (1980, p. 124) notes, many of the debates forget that all science is inherently comparative. The fundamental epistemological principles of control and verification of causal relationships are common to all methods used in the empirical social sciences.

This argument maintains that there is a fundamental continuity between methods. While experiments are distinct because it is possible to manipulate variables,[2] between statistical and comparative methods "there is no such unambiguous dividing line" (Lijphart, 1975, 159–160). Smelser (1976) sees in the comparative method an approximation of statistics. Frendreis (1983) argues that all methods are based on covariation. "Comparative studies"— that is, cross-country analyses—are often based on statistics, so that a comparative *perspective* or *strategy* does not presuppose a distinctive comparative *method* (Benjamin, 1977; Lijphart, 1975; Pennings, Keman, & Kleinnijenhuis, 2007). Comparative studies often rely on statistical research designs, with many cases and quantitative variables. In this broad definition, the comparative method is nothing other than the statistical method applied to designs involving cross-country analyses.

Indeed, for some the specificity of the comparative method lies uniquely in its *goals*: "comparativists are interested in identifying the similarities and differences among macrosocial units" (Ragin, 1987, p. 6). The distinctive aspect is the analysis of countries, societies, civilizations. In the past "comparative politics" (particularly in the United States) used to designate studies on "other" countries. Even today, comparison is often synonymous with either (1) cross-country studies or (2) studies in which the macrosocietal level is used as a control variable in individual-level designs (Przeworski & Teune, 1970). Comparison has for long simply meant the presence of attributes at the level of societies in explanatory statements. This specific goal sets a broad sense of the comparative method, simply as cross-societal analysis through a variety of methods (Easthope, 1974).

An alternative to this "practical" definition points to the *methodological consequences* of research questions with macrosocietal units as cases. It is argued that the comparative method is best suited to answer research questions in which a *low number of cases* are involved (the "small-N problem"). Besides being more "methodological," this alternative has also the advantage of not confining the scope of the comparative method to cross-societal designs. The comparative method can be employed to analyze various types of units: territorial units more generally, but also organizations (such as trade unions, parties, social movements) and individuals. Yet this definition, too, misses to establish a clear dividing line (other than the "N") with other methods.

Does a *distinct* comparative method exist at all? If methods share all major principles and resemble one another "in all respects except one [the N]" (Lijphart, 1971, p. 684), why speak of a comparative method? In recent years, three distinctive aspects have been stressed:

- First, its reliance on *Mill's first three canons* (Method of Agreement, Method of Difference, and the Joint Method) and Boolean algebra dealing with "qualities" rather than degrees ("quantities"). (Incidentally, this should clarify the frequent terminological overlap between "comparative" and "qualitative.")
- Second, an acceptation of causation based on *necessary and sufficient conditions*.
- Third, the *combinatorial or configurational* nature of explanatory models.

Comparison and Statistics

On the basis of these distinctive aspects a "comparative method" has progressively separated from statistics. Through this separation, the comparative method becomes not simply statistics applied to cross-country analyses but a different method from statistics. In recent years this alternative method has been labeled—and identified with—*"the" comparative method*. Obviously, comparative research is still carried out with statistics in broad large-scale designs (what we have called here a *comparative strategy* or *perspective*). Yet a distinct method was developed using other techniques (Mill's first three methods and Boolean algebra), a different understanding of causality (based on necessary and sufficient conditions), and a stress on combinatorial or configurational relationship between independent variables (as opposed to a purely additive type of relationship).

It appears, however, that the commonalities with statistics are stronger than the proponents of this new "comparative method" assume. First, statistical techniques are well able to deal with "qualitative," categorical, discrete, dummy, and dichotomous data (not only in contingency tables but also, and most importantly, through *log-linear analysis*, *logistic regression*, and *probit models* that are treated in more depth in other books of the QASS series; see Aldrich & Nelson, 1984; DeMaris, 1992; Hardy, 1993; Ishii-Kuntz, 1994; Kant Borooah, 2001; Knoke & Burke, 1980; Liao, 1994; Menard, 2001; Pampel, 2000). Second, many statistical techniques are well equipped to deal with combinatorial and configurational explanatory designs (through *interaction effects*, most notably in contingency tables but also in regression analyses; see in particular Jaccard & Wan, 1996; Jaccard & Turrisi, 2003 in this series).

That is to say that between the often juxtaposed "quantitative" and "qualitative" techniques there is *little difference in the fundamental principles*. The focus of this book is on what in the recent years has come to be equated with "the" comparative method. This focus will highlight the strengths and the specificities of the narrow definition of the comparative method—namely, *its capacity to deal with few cases and differentiate between necessary and sufficient conditions*. The book concentrates on what is specific to this kind of comparison as opposed to the broader definition that includes also large-scale comparative strategies between countries based on statistical designs. Yet throughout the book, references to the large-scale statistical techniques will be made (1) to stress the commonalities between comparative and statistical methods and (2) to highlight which aspects of statistics are most relevant for cross-national comparison. First, however, a brief overview of the origins of comparative inquiry is in order.

CHAPTER 2. HISTORY

Origins of the Logic of Comparative Inquiry

Reviewing the development of the role of comparison in the social sciences is important as it stresses the similarities and the common roots of statistical and comparative methods. Reflection on comparison is closely related to its role in the very *logic of scientific inquiry*. The history of "comparison" overlaps, up to a certain time, with that of science and logic.

Two views of comparison dominate this debate. First, in the Cartesian perspective (*La Logique de Port-Royal*, 1662) comparison establishes if something is more or less, better or worse. The emphasis is on continuous *quantities* and *degrees*. Second, in Locke's tradition (*An Essay Concerning Human Understanding*, 1690) the emphasis is on the discrete *absence/ presence* of attributes. In the 17th century, the German school of statistics developed this *qualitative* meaning where "statistics" indicates what today would go under "comparative method." Only later Hegel (*Wissenschaft der Logik*, 1816) unifies the two meanings, with the absence/presence of attributes becoming the two limits of a continuum.

For positivist thinkers in the 19th century to compare means to establish causality on the model of experimental research. John Herschel's *Preliminary Discourse on the Study of Natural Philosophy* (1830) provides the first rules, but it is John Stuart Mill in *A System of Logic* (1843) who proposes the famous "canons" for establishing causal relationships.

With the *Method of Agreement*, if there is only one circumstance always present (cases agree) when a phenomenon occurs while all other are either present or absent (cases disagree), then it can be inferred that this is the cause of the phenomenon. With the *Method of Difference* if there is only one circumstance that is present when the phenomenon is present and is absent when the phenomenon is absent, while all other circumstances are either always present or absent, then it can be inferred that this is the cause of the phenomenon. The *Joint Method of Agreement and Difference* combines these two methods,[3] whereas with the *Method of Concomitant Variations* if a circumstance varies proportionally with a given phenomenon (e.g., "the more . . . , the more . . . "), then it can be inferred that a causal relationship exists.

Mill was convinced that his methods could not be applied to the social sciences (nor to biology) because it is impossible to control for all variables and isolate the cause. However, in biology, Charles Darwin (*On the Origin of Species*, 1859) demonstrated that Mill's methods are useful without the need to control for *all* variables. In sociology, Émile Durkheim (*Les Règles de la Méthode Sociologique*, 1895) thought that the Method of Concomitant Variations (which he labeled "comparative") was the only one not requiring the control of all variables. This is not correct (because this method too requires control to avoid spurious relationships) but leads him nonetheless to put forward the quantitative acceptation of comparison.

In Durkheim's wake the discrete logic is abandoned in favor of quantitative measurement. Authors such as Nagel (1950) and Lazarsfeld (1955; see also Blalock & Blalock, 1968) develop a new method for the social sciences claiming that qualitative measurements should be transformed into *dummy variables* with operational values of 0 and 1 (Hempel & Oppenheim, 1948; Lazarsfeld, 1937; Lazarsfeld & Barton, 1951). This approach drops the term "comparison," which, residually, remains confined to qualitative measurements. It is therefore only recently that "comparative" and "statistical" are distinguished as separate.

Yet, although this distinction has since the 1960s and 1970s been generally accepted (Lijphart, 1971; Smelser, 1966), ambiguities persist. Perhaps most importantly, all methods are based on a common underlying logic codified in Mill's canons.[4] And for Mill himself, ultimately, all of them boil down to the Method of Difference (Mill, 1875, pp. 464–466).[5]

Early Applications in the Social Sciences

These different meanings of comparison—and so also their commonalities—appear in early social studies. Smelser's (1976) book on Tocqueville, Durkheim, and Weber highlights the *variety* of comparative studies (p. 4). Whereas for Tocqueville and Weber there is a distinct comparative method, for Durkheim it equals statistics.

Mill, in his 1840 review of *De la Démocratie en Amérique*, notes that Tocqueville is the first to use systematically his methods. One of Tocqueville's strategies was to identify two sets of characteristics of two nations with the claim that differences in one set could be explained by differences in the other. In Britain, social classes are less isolated from one another than in France causing less group conflict. Sometimes such comparisons are done by using a single unit over time, or by adding a third varying case to strengthen an explanation (Smelser, 1976, pp. 22–30). These strategies follow the Methods of Agreement and Difference.

Weber is the first to distinguish explicitly experimental, statistical, and comparative methods (*Economy and Society*, chap. 1; 1; 6). First, he considered *experiments* possible only in some psychological studies. Indeed, up to the present social psychology is the one field in the social sciences in which experiments take place. Second, *statistical methods* should be limited to mass phenomena. This applies particularly to the subfields of microsociology and demography. Third, Weber sees *comparison* (*die Vergleichung*) as the best option for most empirical sociological analyses. Comparison—in Weber's meaning—applies primarily to macrosociology, anthropology, political science, and international relations. This method consists of comparing the largest possible number of instances that, while otherwise similar, differ in the *one decisive point*. Even though the idea that it is possible to find one decisive difference is an illusion, for Weber, as for Mill, the Method of Difference is the crucial one and all methods can be reduced to this one (a fourth method, the "imaginary experiment," also falling in this category).

For Durkheim, finally, when experiments are not possible the only recourse is "indirect comparison," that is, the statistical method (*Les Règles de la Méthode Sociologique*). He rejected the Methods of Agreement and Difference because he thought that *all* "third" variables need to be controlled for, which obviously is impossible. To establish cause–effect relationships he saw the Method of Concomitant Variations as the only appropriate one. *Le Suicide* is an application of his methodological positions.

CHAPTER 3. SPECIFICITY

In Weber's wake, Smelser (1966; see also Smelser, 1973, 1976) adopted the threefold subdivision of methods, and the comparative method has since been "one of the basic methods . . . of establishing general empirical propositions" (Lijphart, 1971, p. 682; see also Jackman, 1985). What must be stressed here is that, in spite of this trichotomy, all methods are based on common methodological principles. All methods involve variable analysis: (1) establishing *associations* between phenomena (experimental or operational independent variables, and dependent variables) while (2) other factors are *controlled for*.[6] In other words, in all methods researchers "cross-tabulate" (Lazarsfeld, 1955, p. 115).

Experimental, Statistical, and Comparative Methods

Even though the three methods indicated by this trichotomy are not mutually exclusive and, in fact, the trichotomy itself has been criticized (see the end of this section), it has been widely used throughout the development of the social sciences by authors such as Weber, Smelser, and Lijphart. What follows briefly reviews this classification.

Experimental Method

As Parsons (1949) notes, the "experiment is . . . nothing but the comparative method where the cases to be compared are produced . . . under controlled conditions" (p. 743). Control occurs through the deliberate manipulation of variables' values.

The distinctive feature of the experimental method is the possibility to *artificially modify the values of variables*. For some, in addition, the critical feature of an experiment is the random assignment of subjects to treatment. This method draws its strength for assessing causal relationships from the manipulation of operational variables while simultaneously keeping constant the values of other variables. This allows artificial *isolation* of the variables under investigation leading to maximum control. The comparison of outcomes, when variables take different scores, is a central feature of experiments.

Experimental research designs are rare in the social sciences. In most cases it is impossible to modify artificially the values of phenomena. In some specific fields *quasi-experimental* conditions can be created by juxtaposing two groups of individuals, the first of which (the *experimental*

9

group) is exposed to a stimulus while the other (the *control* group) is not. The comparison of the two groups allows one to test the impact of the stimulus. Drawing from different subdisciplines, quasi-experimental research designs are typical of social psychology (e.g., the differentiated effect of medical treatments on a control and an experimental group of patients), but quasi-experiments have been performed also in other fields of the social sciences: in political science (the impact of propaganda levels on the voting behavior of two or more groups of voters), in sociology (factors affecting working conditions in factories such as light, colors, breaks, dress codes—with tie or without—and so on), in economics (the impact of marketing/communication strategies on groups of consumers, the impact of prices on the evaluation of products, etc.), and in anthropology (the differentiated effect of climatic changes—deforestation—on social behavior within tribes). On experimental designs see Brown and Melamed (1990) and Levin (1999) in this same series.

Statistical Method

When researchers cannot manipulate artificially phenomena to make them vary, then the control of variation relies on *different cases* with different values of the variables under investigation. Control and explanation occur through variation. As for experimental and comparative methods, the impact of an independent variable on the dependent variable is established through their *association*. In experiments, researchers look for associations between the change in the values on the dependent variable when the values of independent variables are modified. In the statistical method, researchers look for the association between the values of two or more variables across cases.

Again, the *control of "third" variables* is obtained by keeping constant factors one suspects influence the relationship of interest. Since this cannot be done by keeping artificially factors constant, control is obtained by dividing cases in groups with similar values. To eliminate the impact of age from the relationship between level of education and political participation (younger generations have higher levels of education, which could lead to a spurious relationship) the sample is divided into groups of age and the relation between education and participation is then tested within each group.

Comparative Method

Lijphart (1975) noted that "[t]he comparative method is . . . nothing but the statistical method under relatively unfavorable, but improvable, circumstances" (p. 163). This again points to commonalities between methods.

- First, as for the other two methods, comparative explanations are based on the *association* between variables. For example, Brenner's article on the agrarian structure in preindustrial Europe explains varying levels of economic change through the growth of serfdom in the East and its decline in the West (Skocpol, 1984a, p. 381).

- Second, as in the experimental and statistical method, the comparative method *controls* for the influence of "third" variables by dividing cases in groups with similar values to eliminate their influence from the relationship under inquiry.

It is often claimed that the specificity of the comparative method with respect to the statistical method is that, rather than being based on associations in the form of "the more . . . , the more . . . ," "the more . . . , the less . . . ," and so on, it relies on dichotomous data (presence/absence of phenomena) and thus on Mill's *first three methods of inductive inference*: Method of Agreement, Method of Difference, and the Joint Method. Scholars working in this approach claim that it is therefore a more robust method for designs that face the "unfavorable circumstances" of running out of cases. It must be noted once again, however, that commonalities with statistical techniques are strong in this case too. Statistics has in recent years developed increasingly efficient techniques to deal with dichotomous and categorical variables. In addition, it has been claimed that these methods have the advantage of being better suited to deal with designs in which the number of cases is too small to permit systematic control by means of partial correlations (Lijphart, 1971, p. 684). In this case, too, differences have been overstated. In fact, the debate rather points to two different traditions of comparative research, as noted earlier. One based on large-N statistical and quantitative designs applied to cross-country analyses in a comparative perspective. The other based on small-N logical and qualitative designs. This distinction is discussed in the next section.

To conclude, two caveats should be stressed again. The first is that these three methods, although they have been separated by subsequent authors as distinct, are not mutually exclusive. Often, for example, (quasi-) experimental data is analyzed through statistical techniques. The second is that statistical techniques are often used in a comparative setting—for example, when survey data or voting behavior are analyzed in cross-country perspectives. This does not mean that we are using a distinct method.

Types of Comparison: Large-N and Small-N

The association between *method* and *goals* is however a very close one because the limited number of cases is linked to the research question. In recent decades, with the development of social science and data-collection techniques the number of "cases" has increased.

This has led to a bifurcation of comparative studies into (1) large-scale "macroanalytical" comparative studies based on statistical techniques and (2) small-scale "contrast-oriented" comparative studies based on two-to-five cases typically (Evans-Pritchard, 1963, p. 22; Skocpol & Somers, 1980). During this process comparative analysis has branched in two different directions.

First, the behavioralist rupture with past institutional/historical holistic comparisons led to *quantification* as a general language (that of numbers), *large-scale comparisons*, and *individual data* to be analyzed by *statistical techniques*. This approach is today labeled "large-N" *variable-oriented research*. The expectation of a modernizing convergence of world's social systems toward the Western model led to thinking that everything would become "comparable". The belief that world's societies could be analyzed using universal categories operationalized through quantitative indicators was reinforced by the computer revolution and the possibility to run statistical analyses of a large amount of machine-readable data. These studies are "comparative" in that they analyze different societies, cultures, civilizations, and political systems but, methodologically, they are statistical analyses.

Second, the diversification of societies and political systems—rather than their convergence—that could be observed from the 1960s onward led scholars back to more limited (grounded) comparisons in homogeneous areas with fewer cases. A renewed attention to the social and political context meant the return to *qualitative* (i.e., discrete, categorical, nominal, and dichotomous) levels of measurement, *small-scale comparisons*, and *historical and institutional data,* which could not be analyzed through statistics. New techniques thus developed based on Mill's logic and Boolean algebra. This approach is today labeled "small-N" *case-oriented research* because it puts more weight on whole cases rather than single variables.

Large-Scale Comparative Studies

Writings on "comparative methodology" developed in parallel to the development of new fields of *comparative survey analysis* and *multi-* or *cross-national research*. Increased efforts in the 1950s and 1960s to organize cross-country research, both in the United States and Europe, led to international social science cooperation with the creation of international research groups. The effect of this development has been an *increase of the number of countries* (the "N") and the development of studies based on many cases.

Large-N comparative studies are based on statistical research designs.[7] As mentioned, the label "comparative" refers here not so much to a distinct method, but rather to the presence of countries in the research design, which, however, are treated as "contextual" variables, meaning *attributes at the level of nation-states or societies in explanatory statements*. The macrosocietal level of countries is used as a *control variable* (or residual variable) in individual-level explanatory statements

(Przeworski & Teune, 1970; Teune & Ostrowski, 1973). In large-scale comparative studies, the comparative method is intended broadly as a research strategy based on statistical designs, which includes a large number of countries. This *broad definition* of the comparative method stresses the design (the balance between the number of variables and cases, problems of comparability of indicators and data, etc.) rather than specific logical procedures.

The fact that the label "comparative method" came to designate a specific technique does not imply that comparative analysis cannot be done using statistical techniques. Quite to the contrary, many of the most important comparative studies are of statistical nature and one of the most influential books on comparison (Przeworski & Teune, 1970) is a book on the use of statistics for comparative purposes. In this case, however, the label "comparative method," rather than distinguishing a separate method, indicates the inclusion in statistical research designs of properties—either as operational or control variables—at the level of countries as units of observation.

Statistical techniques such as contingency tables, analysis of variance, factor analysis, correlation, multiple regression, log-linear analysis, and so on are often employed in comparative (i.e., *cross-country* or, more generally, *cross-sectional*) studies. The purpose of this book is not to review all statistical techniques that can be employed for such analyses.[8] Suffice it to say that statistical designs involving cross-sectional analyses can be carried out in two main ways:

- With *individual-level cases*. Data for individuals (e.g., in a survey) are broken down by country (or some other cross-sectional level) with the aggregate cross-sectional level being either an intervening variable or a control variable (e.g., if we investigate the impact of religious affiliation on views on abortion in different countries and wish to establish if the relationship holds true in countries with different traditions of integrating immigrants). In such an example "countries" are not important as such (as "proper names") but as *variables* (as they represent scores in the type of integration traditions).
- With *cross-sectional cases*. Data are collected for some cross-sectional (territorial) units, such as countries, and statistical analyses are run with countries as cases (which is possible if the number of cases is large enough). An example would be the analysis of the impact of labor regulations on unemployment levels in, say, the 30 OECD (Organization for Economic Cooperation and Development) countries. Here again "countries" are important as they represent variation in the scores of labor regulations and levels of unemployment.

A survey analysis in one country would not be considered comparative. If the survey, however, covers two or more countries, it becomes "comparative" in this sense. This does not mean that it uses a distinct "comparative method." It is a statistical design in a cross-country setting. Similarly, a statistical analysis of 150 countries with quantitative data may be labeled "comparative" even though it is based on statistical techniques. In both cases we will speak of a comparative *perspective* or *strategy* but not of a comparative *method*.

Small-Scale Comparative Studies

A large part of comparative research is based on a specific method—called "comparative"—which is distinct from statistics. Many comparative investigations analyze small numbers of cases. This is related to the research question. In many fields the number of empirical cases is too small for statistical inferences: "[i]nstances of social revolution are few" (Ragin, 1987, p. 11).[9] Authors dealing with research questions in which only few cases are available have separated the comparative *method* from large-scale comparative *studies*. This literature identifies a *distinct method*—not simply the "poor cousin" of other methods. Contrary to large-scale comparative studies, here we have a narrow definition of the comparative method. What is stressed is not the design but rather a specific logical procedure based on necessary and sufficient conditions, Mill's methods and Boolean algebra. Whereas large-scale comparative scholars identify the comparative method with statistics applied to designs with a high number of cases, small-scale comparative scholars identify the comparative method with logical or Boolean algebra applied to few cases.

In her study on revolutions, for example, Skocpol identifies a specific comparative logic distinct from multivariate statistical methods for large-scale comparisons (Skocpol, 1979, pp. 36–37; 1984a, pp. 378–379). Similarly, Ragin contrasts (1) the "case-oriented" *comparative method* to (2) the "variable-oriented" approach (Ragin, 1987, chap. 3 and 4; Ragin & Zaret, 1983). The label "comparative method" is reserved to the case-oriented approach identified with the Methods of Agreement and Difference, whereas the latter equals statistics. With this approach small-N studies acquire a new methodological status and are no longer seen as "imperfect" statistical designs.

Intensive and Extensive Research Designs

The difference between large- and small-N comparative designs lies ultimately in the balance between number of variables and number of cases.

A research design that concentrates on few cases and many variables is an *intensive* comparative study. A research design that includes few variables with a high number of cases is an *extensive* type of analysis. This opposition between *intensive* and *extensive research strategies* appears in the following *data matrix*:

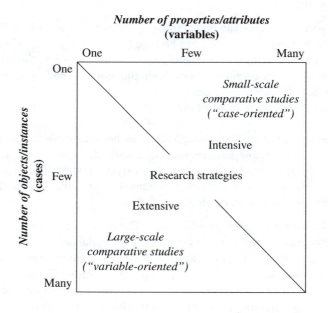

It is important to signal that a debate is currently taking place. "Case-oriented" approaches claim a number of advantages over statistical techniques: a more in-depth type of analysis as a reaction against what is seen as a reductive variable-oriented approach in which cases are split into variables the particular configuration of *whole cases* is neglected. However, there is no consensus on whether case-oriented techniques allow a better handling of nominal and "dummy" variables than multivariate statistics (Goldthorpe, 1997a, 1997b). Statistical techniques have in recent times greatly progressed in this respect. The critique against case-oriented approaches also denounces a return to the past (the various points of this debate are mentioned in Chapter 8 and in the Conclusion).

CHAPTER 4. CASES AND VARIABLES

Case Selection

Units of Analysis

Comparative studies can be based on *as many cases* as wished. Furthermore, the comparative method can be used for *any type* of unit of analysis. There is no logical limitation in applying the comparative method. Logical procedures are independent from both the number and type of units compared.

There are four main types of units:

1. *Individual units.* Even though it has not been done often, it is possible to apply the comparative method to individuals, for example in the study of leadership (communication styles of statesmen, the impact on party cohesion of subsequent leaders, the personality of revolutionary leaders, etc.).

2. *Territorial (cross-sectional) units.* These are the "typical units" of comparative analysis. Geographical and spatial units include various levels of government: local government (communes, counties), provinces or regions, federated units (U.S. states, German *Länder*), nation-states. Territorial units can be defined according to *nonobjective properties* rather than *objective* boundaries or by the data itself. Max Weber analyzes why capitalism has developed in the West and not in the East. Within nations he compares Catholic and Protestant areas.

3. *Functional units.* Comparisons are often carried out on groups, movements or organizations. Such comparisons concern political parties or tribes, trade unions, lobbies and interest groups or family structures (within or across nations). A comparative research design would, for example, compare the structure of the pacifist and feminist movements in a given country, or the ideology of two or more green parties across countries. Functional units can also include international organizations (the European Union compared with North American Free Trade Agreement, the International Monetary Fund compared with the World Bank), groups of consumers in market analyses or tribes in anthropological studies.

4. *Temporal units.* Insofar as temporal units are concerned one should first distinguish between *time points* and *time periods* (Bartolini, 1993, pp. 147–153). To take examples from economics, if one compares inflation levels at "*t*" and "*t* + 1," the comparison is between time points. If one compares inflation before and after the introduction of the common currency in Europe (the euro), the comparison is between periods. The second distinction is between *objective* and *nonobjective* units, as for cross-sectional units. Objective means that the period is determined by the data itself: legislatures, periods between party congresses, censuses, etc. In cases in which data do not offer objective criteria, they can be *aggregated according to a property or variable* (periodization variable) with homogeneous values in each period. Problems of aggregation arise when not all variables can be measured for the same temporal units.

Time adds a further *dimension of variation*. What are compared are the values of shared attributes across cases. With *trend and longitudinal data*, each property or variable takes a different value for each individual or cross-sectional case at different points in time or for different periods. Time points or time periods are treated in the exact same way as individual or cross-sectional units (Bartolini, 1993, p. 146). "Growth," in developmental or sequential generalizations, means values that increase from one time point to the next.

Research designs can therefore be classified not only into large- or small-scale comparative studies but also into *synchronic and diachronic (longitudinal) comparative studies*:

- *Synchronic:* Values of cross-sectional, functional or individual cases are measured for only one point in time or for one period.
- *Diachronic:* Values of cross-sectional, functional or individual cases are measured for different points in time or for different periods.

As seen above, a research design can be intensive (few cases and many variables) or extensive (many cases and few variables). Each, in addition, can be either synchronic or diachronic.

Time as a dimension of variation has often been invoked as a means to increase the number of cases to counter the "small-N problem." This is often done to allow for the use of statistical techniques. Longitudinal analyses have also the advantage of comparing cases within the same context and therefore with many properties controlled for (Lijphart, 1971, 1975).

This "case-stretching" or "multiplicative N-extender" (Lijphart, 1975; Sigelman, 1977), however, is problematic as multiple time-point observations should not be considered separate cases because they are not independent from one another.

Time: Variables, Historical Multicollinearity, Diffusion

Three main issues are related to cases when used in diachronic comparative studies.

1. *Time as a variable.* First, temporal *cases* (units of observation) should not be confused with temporal *variables* (units of variation). This is particularly important in historical comparative research. Take as an example a research design in which the dependent variable is the timing of democratization. According to a frequent operationalization the timing can be "early" (e.g., Britain) or "late" (e.g., Russia). The dependent variable is temporal and the "early" and "later" are its two ordinal values. Temporal variables can also be independent variables. For example, one may want to explain the timing of democratization by using as an explanatory factor the sequence with industrialization (if industrialization occurs before nation-building, then democratization is less likely to take place early).

Examples of temporal variables are below:

Variable	Values
Timing	Early/late
Sequence	Before/after
Pace	Fast/slow

2. *Historical multicollinearity.* Second, the use of longitudinal data can lead to historical multicollinearity when the units of analysis are time points or periods (time series) and the variables are strongly associated with one another (Bartolini, 1993, pp. 157–160; Thrupp, 1970). The relationship between variables is "spurious" because of a general factor of temporal change. This risk is high when dealing with broad socioeconomic and political variables that tend to vary in parallel over time. Since the Industrial Revolution all main socioeconomic indicators tend to increase over time. As Bartolini (1993) notes,

[i]f . . . trends (independent and dependent ones) over time are all associated in a general process of change which is characterised by the existence of a

parallel sheaf of phenomena which are highly interlinked and therefore highly inter-correlated, most factors associated with the general change would . . . be also associated with the dependent variable. (p. 158)

With temporal cases the analysis must therefore focus on the *deviations of this trend in different cross-sectional cases*. Trends should be analyzed in relative terms, that is, where it has occurred earlier or later, faster or slower. This entails a combination of temporal and cross-sectional variation. To do this, researchers resort to "slides of synchronic comparisons through time" (Bartolini, 1993, p. 159, emphasis omitted). One must add a cross-sectional unit variance to a cross-temporal unit variance. Generalizations of the sort "the earlier . . . , the faster . . . " therefore imply that we take into our analysis more than one cross-sectional unit.

3. *Diffusion*. Third, in temporal developments socioeconomic and political phenomena "have time" to spread from one case to the other—be it organizations or territorial units (such as political systems). This leads to the *convergence and similarity of values over time*. Cross-sectional cases are therefore not independent from one another. The problem of diffusion is discussed in the next section on Selection Bias (point 3).

Selection Bias

Selection bias arises from the inclusion in the analysis of a number of cases chosen from a larger pool. There are two types of bias (Geddes, 1990, pp. 132–133):

- First, biased *inference*. The bias arises from "the *non*random selection of cases [that] results in inferences, based on the resulting sample, that are not statistically representative of the population" (Collier, 1995, p. 462). One cannot infer results obtained for a subset of cases to the entire population. This is a problem of *generalization* (*external validity*).
- Second, biased *causality*. The bias results from different subsets of cases that lead to different conclusions concerning causal relationships: different cases, different causes. Cases are overrepresented on one end or the other of the distribution of the dependent variable, and "truncated" on the other end. "Selecting on the dependent variable" leads to an asymmetry among cases with skewed values of the dependent variable (e.g., a selection of countries with only high values of political instability). This is a problem of *specification* (*internal validity*).

In comparative analysis selection bias has five potential causes.

1. *Research design*. The selection of cases concerns the *sample*. If researchers study the entire universe of cases there is no risk of selection bias. In fact, researchers are not "selecting" strictly speaking although even categories such as "Third World" or "industrialized countries" are never entirely objective but entail theoretical constructs.

Concerning *cross-sectional* cases, the most common form of selection bias is selecting cases that have achieved the outcome of the variable to be explained, that is, we exclude "negative cases" (see point 4 below). For example, in a study on electoral reform researchers would only consider countries in which the change from proportional representation (PR) to majoritarian systems (or vice versa) has taken place. The extreme form of such a bias is the selection of only one value of the dependent variable (King, Keohane, & Verba, 1994, p. 130). Selection bias can affect *temporal units*, when arbitrarily selecting specific time points of longer time series. Often analysts select periods of time in which the values of the variable have reached a high or a low point. In this case too the range of variation is truncated. The most common bias here is the focus on *endpoints* of the time series: most recent periods leading to overestimate recent changes (Collier & Mahoney, 1996; Geddes, 1990, pp. 146–147).

This is important for the comparative method as causality is established in some cases with Mill's Method of Agreement—in which cases differ on a large number of properties, sometimes counterfactually (Collier, 1995; Fearon, 1991; Peters, 1998, p. 72)—and researchers select cases in which the outcome is positive (i.e., the event occurs). This is selecting on the dependent variable (cases "agree" on the dependent variable). As Geddes (1990) argues, unless one includes negative cases that "disagree" on the dependent variable, "one cannot know whether or not the factors identified are crucial antecedents of the outcome under investigation" (p. 132). As will be seen below, in this way we cannot establish *sufficient* conditions but only *necessary* ones.

2. *Historical contingency*. The problem of historical contingency concerns the *universe*. The population itself is "self-selected" on the dependent variable. Even studies that include all existing cases, say countries, are not immune from problems of selection bias. The set of real-world cases is biased as a result of "natural" or "historical" contingency, meaning that the pool of cases has been biased by social processes.

Historical contingency leads to the *self-selection* of cases. Choosing the member states of an international organization (Organization for Economic

Cooperation and Development or the European Union) implies that the cases were self-selected by their choice to join the organization (Ebbinghaus, 2005). More radically, if we analyze nation-states we bias our analysis by taking political units that "survived" the natural or historical selection whereas most disappeared (Tilly, 1975a, p. 15). If our dependent variable is state formation, we have only successful cases and no negative ones (i.e., states that "died").

Historical contingency leads also to what Ragin (1987) has labeled *limited variety or diversity* (pp. 25–27, 104–113), that is, cases whose values do not represent the entire possible theoretical range. History did not provide us with all possible combinations. For example, among advanced industrial economies, there is no Protestant country that experienced late democratization.

Consequently, historical contingency has an impact on the inference from samples to population. As a general rule, the criterion by which the sample is created must not be correlated with the dependent variable. However, if at any particular point in time the population includes only cases that "history" or "nature" has selected, then even random samples are selected on the dependent variable. As Geddes (1990) notes, we cannot evaluate the impact of a military innovation on state formation in the 16th century by looking at nation-states that succeeded to survive in the 18th century because all surviving states would have that innovation (p. 135).

3. *"Galton's problem."* First, the *problem.* The 19th-century polymath and anthropologist Francis Galton criticized a comparative research paper by Edward Tylor (1889) on a cross-sectional correlation between two dichotomous variables noting that the outcome was the product of the diffusion across cases rather than the product of a causal relationship between variables. It was an artifact of diffusion rather than a functional connection.

Operationally, diffusion is a "factor" that accounts for the association between the correlated variables (Smelser, 1976, p. 212). The functional association is *spurious* because of the effect of diffusion processes (Lijphart, 1975, p. 171). Statistically, diffusion or contagion processes among cases *violate the assumption of the independence among units of analysis.* Units of analysis—be it organizations or territorial units—are not isolated from one another. In temporal developments phenomena spread from one case to the other. There might therefore be a convergence of values over time.[10]

Most units are open systems subject to external influences: (1) imitation, borrowing, and learning from the practices of others (Ross & Homer, 1976);

(2) exchange or coordination when they belong to some overarching integrating organization; (3) imposition by conquest, colonialism, economic dependency (Moul, 1974); and (4) "societal fission," that is, migrations or splinters from common original system (Strauss & Orans, 1975). The risk is to end up with $N = 1$. Przeworski and Teune (1970) ask, "how many independent events can we observe? If the similarity within a group of systems is a result of diffusion, there is only one independent observation" (p. 52). The degree of freedom is zero. Therefore, "[i]f a unit is not independent, no new information . . . is obtained by studying it twice, and no additional confirmation . . . is obtained by counting it twice" (Zelditch, 1971, pp. 282–283).

The problem increases with transnationalization processes, the amelioration of communication, spread of information, and acceleration of exchanges. "In an increasingly interdependent world, comparative social scientists are beginning to realize that social phenomena . . . are not isolated and self-contained, but rather are affected by domestic events occurring within other societies" (Klingman, 1980, p. 123). With a shrinking world the problem is stronger today than in the past. For example, it is plausible to suppose that the development of welfare states in various countries is affected by diffusion processes (Collier & Messick, 1975). Also Tilly's (1984) critique to Rokkan's model points to its failure in genuinely analyzing the interactions between countries (p. 129).

Second, the *solutions*. These lie within two extremes. One extreme is to "capitulate" (Sztompka, 1988). The world is one single case and research should focus on enclaves of "uniqueness" resisting globalization. The other extreme is not to exaggerate the problem (Blaut, 1977). The term *semidiffusion* (as opposed to *hyperdiffusion*) indicates (1) that some societies are more immune than others to external influences (because of selective adoption, cultural resistance, nonpreparation to innovation) and (2) that diffusion concerns some fields (e.g., monetary policies) but not others (e.g., the ethnic composition of a country).

Between the extremes the following solutions have been put forward:

(a) *Cross-section sampling procedures.* Most solutions try to "control for" the variable "diffusion" through case selection (Naroll, 1961, 1964, 1965, 1968; Naroll and D'Andrade, 1963; Wellhofer, 1989). Solutions to Galton's problem in anthropology—where the problem has first been confronted—is to choose societies that are not connected to one another and where diffusion is unlikely. This is equivalent to "most different systems design" (MDSD). Cases are selected from different contexts. The choice of cases assures their independence. This, however, is problematic in modern industrialized societies (Moul, 1974; Peters, 1998, pp. 41–43).

(b) *Evaluating diffusion possibilities*. This solution suggests to detect interdependence through "diffusion possibility matrices" (Pryor, 1976), which include measures of potential diffusion between pairs of societies. These measures are based on factors like language similarity and geographical proximity (Ross & Homer, 1976). Diffusion possibility matrices provide a contextual variable to be included as a control factor. Similar is the use of international dependence indices (e.g., Trade Composition Index).

(c) *Time series analysis*. For some, Galton's problem is ultimately a phenomenon of statistical dependence between cases. The solution is to include the process of diffusion in the analysis, that is, to "model" interdependence in regression analyses (Goldthorpe, 2000, p. 56; Klingman, 1980). Time series analysis is able to incorporate across-system diffusion effects, that is, the spatial diffusion of the dependent variable from system to system. This, however, does not apply to small-N designs.

4. *The choice of "negative" cases*. Biased results can also occur from the choice of negative cases. Only recently has this problem received the attention it deserves. How do researchers decide about a negative case, that is, a "nonevent?" "Where and when do 'nonsocial revolutions' occur?" (Mahoney & Goertz, 2004, p. 653). Negative cases are important for two reasons. First, they affect the balance in the frequency distribution between positive and negative cases. It makes either positive or negative cases more or less "rare." Second, different cases lead to different causes. The inclusion or exclusion of cases might affect results because cases have different values (internal validity).

The choice is between treating a case as negative (nonrevolution, nonwar) or as irrelevant. A negative case is part of the sample of cases of the analysis. An irrelevant case is not an instance under investigation. If we were to explain the participation to the Allied coalition in World War II we may include Switzerland as a case of nonparticipation, whereas Bolivia would be an irrelevant case. Its inclusion would introduce an additional negative case into the population, risking an overrepresention of negative cases. In contrast, the exclusion of too many negative cases is also a source of bias because it overrepresents positive cases.

The "Possibility Principle" provides a guide in treating a case as either positive or negative. According to this principle, "only cases where the outcome of interest is *possible* should be included in the set of negative cases; cases where the outcome is *impossible* should be relegated to a set of uninformative and hence irrelevant observations" (Mahoney & Goertz, 2004, p. 653). Skocpol (1984a) too suggests that negative cases should be as similar as possible to positive cases in all respects except for their value on the dependent variable. Similarly, Ragin (2000) argues that "[n]egative cases should resemble positive cases in as many ways as possible, especially with respect to the commonalities exhibited by the positive cases" (p. 60); see also Ragin (1997).

The "Possibility Principle" formalizes these views (Mahoney & Goertz, 2004, pp. 657–658):

- *Possibility principle:* Choose as negative cases those where the outcome is possible.
- *Rule of inclusion:* Cases are relevant if their value on at least one independent variable is positively related to the outcome of interest.
- *Rule of exclusion:* Cases are irrelevant if their value on any eliminatory independent variable predicts the nonoccurrence of the outcome of interest. This rule takes precedent over the "Rule of Inclusion."

5. *"Biased" selection of historical sources*. Finally, also the inaccurate use of "history as a database" to test hypotheses can lead to selection bias. The problem lies in the selection of secondary historiographic sources. Often comparative political sociology relies on the work of historians for their data where "past events [are] ready to be coded" (Lustick, 1996, p. 605). However, among comparative historical sociologists there is no consensus on how to use second-hand sources of evidence (Skocpol, 1984a, p. 382).

Historical data entail implicit theories about past events. Researchers run the risk of selecting sources that include accounts of past events they are likely to find most useful because they are "in tune" with the typology or theory they are developing. There is a risk of treating interpretations as "factual" accounts of historical events and processes. In many cases, sociologists "enjoy a delightful freedom to play 'pick-and-mix' in history's sweetshop" (Goldthorpe, 1991, p. 225; see also Goldthorpe, 1994).

The quarrel on "What Are Historical Facts?" (the phrase is from Carl Becker's 1926 paper), whether they are *discovered or constructed*— objective or subjective—is an old one. Max Weber and Leopold von Ranke promoted a "scientific" analysis of historical documents and archives. This was continued by the French social historians of the *Annales* after

World War II. Solutions to biased historical sources can only come from awareness and rigor: make the theoretical choice of a particular type of source explicit and adopt a wide theoretical range of sources in order to avoid any bias—in particular by identifying areas of overlap between different sources (Lustick, 1996, pp. 613–616).

Variables and the Property Space

Levels of Measurement

The levels of measurement that are distinguished in the social science disciplines are (1) *nominal, dichotomous, or categorical variables* (e.g., different types of family structures: nuclear family, childless family, single-parent family, extended family, etc.), (2) *ordinal variables* (e.g., the international role of countries: strong, influent, weak, insignificant), and (3) *interval or ratio-scale variables* (e.g., gross national product, or GNP, per capita, age, salary, party membership, etc.). While the first two levels of measurement are usually labeled "qualitative" the third level is considered "quantitative." Information not only allows one to establish which case is "more or less" but also by "how much."

Large-scale research designs involving a high number of cases and quantitative variables are best dealt with through statistical methods, which, as mentioned, are also able to handle nominal, dichotomous, and categorical variables when the number of cases is sufficiently high. However, relationships based on a limited number of cases are problematic to establish between quantitative variables as well. For this reason, they are sometimes collapsed into multicategory variables (two categories in case of dichotomous variables, or more categories) to allow for the use of Mill's methods and Boolean algebra. The same applies to nominal or categorical variables. Also, in some cases, we are more interested in establishing whether a given factor is a sufficient or necessary condition for a phenomenon to occur. In this case too, Mill's methods and Boolean algebra are more indicated. This requires, however, that the level of measurement is changed, indeed collapsed in dichotomous variables, that is, in binary base 2 (values of 0/1) where 1 indicates the *presence* of a given property and 0 its *absence*. The presence/absence of attributes follows a qualitative and discrete logic rather than a quantitative/continuous logic based on degree and size.

Two major problems are related to collapsing quantitative or ordinal levels of measurement into categorical ones. First, with the transformation of interval- or ratio-scale variables (e.g., GNP per capita) into multicategory dichotomous variables, there is a degree of *information loss*. In the table below we do not know what the difference between Spain, Italy, and Greece is (namely around $15,000, $18,000, and $12,000, respectively).

Instances (Cases)	Level of GNP Per Capita ($)			
	0–10,000	10,000–20,000	20,000–30,000	30,000–45,000
Spain	0	1	0	0
Italy	0	1	0	0
Greece	0	1	0	0

Second, to establish categories, the researcher is asked to chose *cut-off points*, which have a strong impact on the relationship under investigation (see above the discussion about bias and see the section Beyond Dichotomization: Fuzzy Sets and the Use of Computer Programs in Chapter 7 for a discussion of cut-off points).

With ordinal variables, on the contrary, there is no loss of information. For each category (e.g., the levels of international influence) each case is allocated either the score 0 or 1 on the various levels of international influence.

Instances (Cases)	International Role			
	Strong	Influential	Weak	Insignificant
Iceland	0	0	0	1
United States	1	0	0	0
Russia	0	1	0	0

Data organized in such a way are then used—in small-N designs—to test hypotheses with Mill's methods and with Boolean algebra to establish if the presence/absence of, say, "strong international role" or the presence/absence of one of the four categories of GNP represent a necessary or sufficient condition for a given phenomenon to occur.

Overdetermination and "Degrees of Freedom"

As seen above, the problem that many "comparative" (i.e., cross-national) analyses face is the small number of cases combined with a large number of variables. This problem of "many variables, small N problem"

(Barton, 1955; Lijphart, 1971) means that there are too few cases to test all potentially relevant variables, a problem of *overdetermination* or lack of "degrees of freedom" (Campbell, 1975).[11]

There are two main solutions to the problem of "many variables, small N." The first solution is to *increase the number of cases*. This is what is suggested by Lijphart (1971) who, however, observed also that the more the cases, the larger the property space (the number of variables). This is a well-known *paradox* in comparative studies: increasing the number of cases leads simultaneously to a larger property space and therefore to the need to include yet more cases to compensate for the increase of the property space.

The second solution is to try to *reduce the number of variables*. The research design plays an important role in reducing the number of theoretically relevant variables (King, Keohane, & Verba, 1994, 1995, 119–120).[12] Three main alternatives are available.

1. *Focus on similar cases.* Choosing similar cases on as many important properties as possible allows one to control for a larger number of variables that, as a consequence, are excluded from the analysis. Reducing the range of variation means to *control for* and thus eliminate variables. Increasing the overall number of variables controlled for reduces the number of *operative* variables (dependent and independent) in the explanatory model. However, the by-product of looking for similar cases is the reduction of the number of cases. The paradox works here the other way round: there are less similar cases than dissimilar ones (Lijphart, 1971, p. 687; see "most similar systems design" [MSSD] in Chapter 5).

2. *Focus on "key" variables.* This solution consists of adopting parsimonious explanatory models with as few independent variables as possible. Which "key" variables should be included in the model is a subjective decision by the researcher. The comparative method— as any other method—can afford introducing a larger number of variables only if the number of cases allows it.

3. *Combine variables.* In a "factor-analytical" perspective, to reduce the number of variables it is sometimes possible to combine two or more variables into a single one according to underlying properties.

CHAPTER 5. CONTROL

This chapter deals with two related issues. First, the *comparability* of cases. Second, how it is possible to reduce, and possibly eliminate, the influence of "third variables" on the relationship between independent and dependent variables under investigation, that is, variables the researcher wants to *control* for. Classification and taxonomical treatment underlie both issues. For this reason they have been grouped together in a single chapter.

Comparability: The Limits of Comparison

Comparative researchers are often confronted with the problem of what is and what is not comparable. This relates to (1) the *limits* of comparison and (2) the *strategies* for making cases comparable.

Are there *logical limits* to comparison? Are there things that are "too different" to be compared and to be included in the same research design or, on the contrary, is "everything comparable?" Is it possible to compare the election of a U.S. president with the selection of the head of a tribe in the Amazonian jungle? Questions of comparability have important consequences. A *historicist approach* tends to consider phenomena as *unique*. It is the supposed "uniqueness" of events that makes them noncomparable. The critique to extended comparisons takes sometimes the form of "ethnocentrism," which maintains that concepts developed in the frame of a given society/time do not fit other cases, and that what we know about some societies cannot be extended to others.

As seen in the definition in Chapter 1, however, with the comparative method we do not compare directly two or more cases. *We compare the values that the common attribute takes for each case*. Let us take, as examples from different subfields in the social sciences, the following statements:

- Crime is higher in suburban areas than in inner city centers.
- Welfare policies of the new government are more restrictive than those of the previous government.
- The electoral system of Brazil is more proportional than the Argentinian system.

First, for each statement there are two objects: urban areas, governments, electoral systems. Second, for each statement there is an attribute that the two objects share: crime rates, welfare policies, the proportionality of the electoral system. What is compared between suburbs and city centers is the rates of crime (operationalized, say, as number of reports to the police). In the second example, levels of "generosity" of welfare policies can be measured through health benefits, pensions, unemployment subsidies, and so on. In the third example, we do not compare electoral systems as such but their proportionality. The Gallagher least square index of disproportionality (Lsq) is 3.70 in Brazil and 13.5 in Argentina. The electoral system in Brazil is therefore more proportional than the Argentinian one.

The question of comparability is therefore one of *sharing common attributes*. What is compared are the values of the cases on these shared properties. From a methodological point of view, therefore, *there are no limits to comparison*. It is possible to compare the duration of "office" between the U.S. president and the head of a tribe. In the former case it is 4 years (renewable once), in the second it is lifelong. We can also compare their selection: by election and birth. When comparing the values of the common attribute (duration of office, method of selection) the level of measurement might be nominal, ordinal, or quantitative. In the comparison of welfare generosity values are quantitative; but in the comparison of the selection of heads of state, values are nominal.

Taxonomical Treatment

The comparability between cases is thus given by *sharing a same attribute or property*. If cases A, B, . . . N share the attribute X, then their values (0, 1, 2, etc.) can be compared. Comparability is obtained by finding a "common denominator" between cases. As Sartori (1970) has put it, "to compare is 'to assimilate,' i.e., to discover deeper or fundamental similarities below the surface of secondary diversities" (p. 1035).

The first step in the logical control procedure is therefore conceptual and consists of defining *empirical universals* making cases comparable (Sartori, 1970, 1984a, 1991). Empirical universals are concepts or categories defining the attribute shared by the cases compared. The transformation of single historical observations into comparable cases is obtained—in a famous phrase—through "*the substitution of variables for proper names*" (Przeworski & Teune, 1970, p. 25; see also Collier, 1991a, 1991b).

This is why a purely "case-oriented" approach is not tenable. Comparison implies variable-thinking, attributes, properties. If this is missing, no comparison is possible: "the rule of holism yields a clear and straightforward contradiction: only incomparables are comparable" (Zeldich, 1971, p. 276). As Bartolini (1993) notes, "[c]ases cannot be compared 'as wholes,' but only when common properties are identified"

(p. 137) (see also Goldthorpe, 1997a, pp. 2–4). Both the so-called "variable-" and "case-oriented" approaches—one relying primarily on statistics and large-N designs; the other on Mill's methods, Boolean algebra, and small-N designs—reason in terms of variables and are interested in variable analysis. This again stresses similarities between the two traditions of comparative studies.

Classification and Typologization

Classification allows one to establish which cases are comparable, that is, share a common attribute (Kalleberg, 1966). By establishing what is similar, what belongs to a same group of cases or class, one establishes whether or not they share an attribute and can be compared.

1. *Equivalence.* Comparable means something that shares a same attribute (electoral turnout, animist rituals), that is, belongs to a same class of cases. If we wish to study electoral turnout in national parliamentary elections, we must first be able to establish which countries can be included and which cannot. If we wish to study animist rituals, we must first be able to establish which cultures have animist rituals and which do not. Comparable is something that has a given degree of "sameness," something that belongs to a same group defined by a shared attribute. To be able to discriminate in that way one must define clearly what is meant by "electoral turnout" or "animist ritual." The concept or category must have the same meaning for all the cases included in the comparison.[13] The category must be *equivalent* (van Deth, 1998). Say, by "electoral turnout" we mean voting in free, recurrent, and correct elections by universal suffrage for a parliament in which more than one party present lists and candidates, and with alternative sources of information. In such a definition one would not include China today. China is therefore not a comparable case.[14]

Before one can investigate the presence or absence of attributes, or before one can rank objects or measure them in terms of some variable, one "must form the concept of that variable" (Lazarsfeld & Barton, 1951, p. 155). The concepts or categories should never be *vague*, that is, they should always indicate *to which empirical aspects they refer.* Empirical *referents* of concepts should always be clearly stated: "by electoral turnout we mean [a number of empirical referents]." Only in this way is it possible to say whether or not a case is indeed a case of turnout. In other terms, it is only through nonvague concepts that one can establish if cases share the same attribute—and ultimately establish their comparability. If the meaning of this concept or category is precise, its *discriminating power* is enhanced, that is, it divides the domain of cases into classes separated by a sharp boundary.

This has important consequences for data collection. Concepts and categories are "data containers" and these should be defined in such a way as to increase their discriminating power, that is, clearly indicate which are cases of turnout and which are not. One can compare levels of political violence in Chile and in Canada only if the same thing is meant in the two cases. One cannot compare political violence in these two cases if in the former case one includes as empirical referents killings, kidnappings, and street violence and in the latter sit-ins, manifestations, and verbal attacks to political leaders.

2. *Logic of classification.* Classification is the most important procedure of *concept formation*: "[it] is the basic type of concept-formation in science. Neither comparison (nonmetrical ordering) nor measurement proper can take place without it . . . Comparison can only be made after classification has been completed" (Kalleberg, 1966, pp. 73, 75). "In short, *two objects being compared must be of the same class*—they must either *have* an attribute or *not*. If they have it, and *only* if they have it, may they be compared as to which has it more and which has it less" (p. 76).

Following Bailey's (1994) definition (in this same series), classification is a general process, as well as the result, of grouping cases in terms of similarity. In establishing groups and classes, we want to minimize differences within each group while maximizing differences between groups. The similarity element defines which objects belong to the same class (genus), whereas the difference element defines what distinguishes classes (species and subspecies).

The classificatory treatment of concepts has three basic rules.

- *Dimensions of classification.* Classifications are based on explicit criteria for the creation of groups. Groups can be based on a single dimension or property (one-dimensional) or based on a number of dimensions (multidimensional). The term *typology* is used for multidimensional classifications in which categories are distinguished conceptually rather than empirically (*taxonomy*).
- *Mutual exclusiveness.* There must be only one class for each item. No case should belong to more than one class. If a classification has a mutually exclusive set of classes, they do not overlap with each other.
- *Joint exhaustiveness.* There must be a class for each case. No case should be left out. If the categories are exhaustive, each case will be

in one of the categories of a variable. A problem sometimes is that, to have a class for each case, classifications tend to have a high number of classes. To avoid that sometimes categories such as "none" or "other" are included.[15]

It is often maintained that one of the specificities of the small-N comparative method is the more extensive use of classification. Its role in comparison is indeed crucial. However, the role of classification is equally important in other methods, namely the large-scale comparison based on quantitative variables and statistical techniques.

Classification precedes statistics; it is not alien to it. Concept formation refers to differences in *kind* rather than *degree* (Sartori, 1970, p. 1036). The taxonomical hierarchy from more general to more specific touches directly on problems of membership in categories and *classification* principles. The *qualitative* logic of *classification* therefore comes before that of *order and quantity*. The logic of gradation belongs to that of classification. Before being able to use the signs "more than" (>) and "less than" (<) one must establish the signs "equal to" (=) and "different from" (≠). Comparability is therefore a problem of "what," a qualitative problem that cannot be replaced by the question of "order" or "how much."

Levels of Generality

1. *Conceptual stretching.* If concepts are able to "travel," then they apply to a large number of comparable cases. However, not all concepts and categories are good at traveling: some are developed in the frame of specific geographical, cultural, and socioeconomic contexts and, when extended to "new" cases, they do not make sense. This problem is particularly acute in cross-national studies. "Western concepts" have a different meaning in other parts of the world. What Sartori (1970) has called the "traveling problem" (p. 1033) is closely related to the "expansion of politics," that is, an objective increase of the number of cases and a subjective increase of interest in sociopolitical issues since the 1960s.

The traveling problem appears when concepts and categories are applied to new cases, different from those around that they had originally been developed. A frequent but inadequate answer to this problem has been "conceptual stretching" (Hempel, 1952; Peters, 1998, pp. 86–93; Sartori, 1970). *Conceptual stretching* refers to the distortion of concepts to make them fit new cases. The stretching arises when *a category developed for one set of cases is extended to additional cases and these new cases are too different and the category is no longer appropriate in its original form* (Collier & Mahon, 1993).

2. *Ladder of abstraction.* How can conceptual stretching be avoided? First, comparative research relies on *empirical universals*, or *observational concepts*, that is, abstractive inferences from empirical observations rather than *theoretical (nonobservational) concepts* such as "system," "feedback," or "equilibrium." These concepts have no empirical referents. They are nonoperationalizable, that is, nonmeasurable.

Second, if we want to increase the number of cases, to avoid conceptual stretching we must simultaneously decrease the characteristics and properties of the empirical concept. This is done by climbing the so-called "ladder of abstraction" (Sartori, 1970, p. 1041, 1984a, p. 24) or "ladder of generality" (Collier & Mahon, 1993). Empirical concepts can be placed at different levels of an imaginary scale. Their vertical positioning on the ladder depends on the relationship between *intension and extension of the concept.*

- *Extension (or denotation):* These terms indicate the set of objects, phenomena, events, or entities to which the concept or category refers. The extension of a concept is the class of "things" to which it applies.
- *Intension (or connotation):* These terms indicate the set of attributes, properties, or characteristics of a concept or category. They define the category and therefore determine the membership of a case to it. The intension of a concept is the class of properties that determine the "things" to which the concept applies.

The relation between extension and intension obeys a *law of inverse variation*: the greater the intension of a concept, the more limited the "things" that belong to this class as defined by the attributes of the concept (Collier & Mahon, 1993). In other words, the richer and longer the list of characteristics of a concept, the more limited the set of objects to which this concept applies. Conversely, the more limited the specification of attributes and properties of a concept, the larger the class of "things" (entities, objects, events) to which the concept refers.

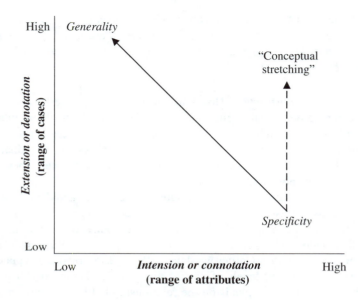

It is possible to compare the selection of the executive in Germany and in the United States insofar as the attribute "selection" applies to both cases. These two cases are comparable insofar as they share an attribute. However, it is not possible to compare the "election" of the executive between these two countries, as in the former the executive is nominated by the parliament and not elected. Comparability therefore depends on the *level of generality* of the language that is applied to observations. "Selection" is more general than "election."

A limited intension of the concept of "executive selection" without specifying attributes covers a larger number of cases. On the contrary, a larger intension, that is, more specifying attributes—such as "direct election by voters"—would exclude a number of cases in which executives are either appointed by the parliament (most European democracies) or are elected indirectly through an electoral college (as in the United States).

There are two ways of climbing the ladder of abstraction. One is by broadening the extension of a concept (a reduction of attributes or properties). The result is a larger class with lesser differentiation but still with clear boundaries and discriminating power. This is the correct way of proceeding. The other is "conceptual stretching," which increases the extension *without* diminishing the intension. The extension is increased by obfuscating the boundaries of the concept (Sartori, 1970, p. 1041).

Family Resemblance and Radial Categories

In discrete categorization, cases either belong to a class or not: they either have an attribute or not (Kalleberg, 1966, p. 76). As Sartori noted, however, the requirement of *positive identification of attributes* may be, in practice, too exacting. His answer to the problem was to say that, when it is not possible to define the exact attributes of a concept, then one must state clearly what the concept *is not*, that is, *a negative identification of attributes* (Sartori, 1970). Two further solutions to the problem posed by discrete boundaries have been proposed: (1) *family resemblance* and (2) *radial categories* (Collier & Mahon, 1993).[16]

1. *Family resemblance.* Family resemblance (originally developed by linguistic philosophers such as Wittgenstein) is based on the principle that, if there is no single attribute that all the members of a category share, researchers can include cases that share the attribute to *varying degrees.* Take, for example, "democracy" defined through

(1) universal suffrage (political rights); (2) free press, association, belief, individual's protection (civil rights); (3) free, recurrent, correct elections; (4) executive responsible before legislative; and (5) independent judiciary.

If we compare Britain, France, Germany, and Belgium in the late 19th century we see that the attribute "democratic" is not perfectly shared by all cases. In Britain there was no universal suffrage, in France the judiciary was not independent, and in Germany the government could not be outvoted by the parliament. With classical categorization only Belgium would fall into the "democracy" category.

The idea of family resemblance is to consider that the attribute is shared to *some degree* by all the cases. The *prototype category* (democracy) is an *analytical construct* with a heuristic usefulness. Max Weber's ideal types are categories that were defined analytically rather than based on attributes shared by empirically observed cases (Burger, 1976). Real cases share with the ideal type its defining attribute to some degree, meaning that the attribute assumes a "varying geometry" across cases. The advantage is that useful categories are not abandoned hastily by being overly strict.

2. *Radial categories.* Radial categories (originally developed by cognitive scientists such as Lakoff) also rely on a "varying geometry" of attributes across cases.

There is a "prototype" or ideal type representing the perfect or more complete case. This is the "primary subcategory" of which "secondary subcategories" are a variation. Secondary subcategories do not include all the properties of the primary one. Noncentral subcategories arise when the component elements of the primary subcategory are taken one-by-one or in different combinations (but not complete). It is different from classical categorization where there is a progressive differentiation into genus (superordinate) and species (subordinate). What differentiates the superordinate category from subordinate categories is that the subordinate categories have *more* properties that are added to the superordinate one to differentiate different types (are more "precise"). In radial categorization what differentiates the secondary from the primary subcategory is that we have *less* component elements.

These classification strategies offer different answers to how we construct categories. This has consequences on comparability, that is, which cases we include in the analysis.

Control and Research Design

The previous section has discussed the importance of classification and taxonomic treatment for matters of *comparability*. Classification has a second important role. Classification allows one to *control for variables* (Smelser, 1976, 167–174). These two roles should not be confused. Comparability concerns *cases*; control concerns *variables*. Once comparability has been established, classification becomes an instrument to exclude factors researchers do not want to influence the relationship under investigation—a process through which unwanted sources of variation are reduced.

Matching and Randomization

Empirical research is based on hypotheses concerning causal relationships between phenomena (or variables, once they have been operationalized). Through tests against empirical evidence hypotheses are either verified or rejected. The empirical test of hypotheses implies two separate but related aspects:

1. determining the *association* between phenomena, that is, between cause and effect (in operational terms the *association between independent and dependent variables*);

2. while *isolating* it from the influence of other variables to establish— one by one—the causal role of each operative variable independently.

The same variable can be an experimental or control variable in different phases of the test depending on whether or not it is "allowed" to vary.

Through the transformation of independent variables in control variables and vice versa for all variables that are considered relevant, the investigator progressively gains confidence in the explanation, refines the theoretical argument, and strengthens results. As for all types of research, which variables should be controlled for is a decision by researchers themselves based on previous knowledge (theory) or new insights.

The control of variables can be carried out through

- *Randomization (control through MDSD)*. With randomization *differences* are excluded: if the same phenomenon occurs in different contexts, it follows that differences do not account for its presence and, thus, are irrelevant. This is similar to MDSD and, as will be seen, to the Method of Agreement. The MDSD eliminates "third variables" for which values vary across cases.
- *Matching (control through MSSD)*. With matching *similarities* are excluded: a variation in the dependent variable cannot be caused by a factor that is constant across cases. Through matching the influence of third variables is excluded by transforming them into constants and thus do not represent an unwanted source of variation. This corresponds to the MSSD and to the Method of Difference. The MSSD eliminates "third variables" for which values are constant across cases.

To *randomize* means to select cases that cover the entire range of values of a given property. Random samples, which assure that each case in the universe (or population) has an equal chance of being drawn, allow one to infer with more confidence. Randomization processes are typical of statistical methods, which can rely on large numbers of cases. To *match* (sometimes called *parameterization, standardization,* or *stratification* in the case of sampling) means to transform variables into *constant* scores that do not vary so that their influence is excluded and the relationship between independent and dependent variables is isolated.

It is important to note that both randomization and matching as techniques for controlling unwanted sources of variation rely on procedures of *case selection*, that is, ultimately on the *research design*.

In the social sciences research designs are particularly important because researchers draw cases from *already existing* data. In experiments, investigators have a direct influence on the *creation* of data (Cook & Campbell, 1979). This is a *situational manipulation*. The transformation of variables into constants to exclude unwanted sources of variation and isolate operative variables can be deliberately carried out in laboratory conditions. However, both the statistical and the comparative methods have no direct influence on the data. Control therefore occurs through *conceptual manipulation.* Investigators *select cases* either with similar values on a given property (which they want to keep constant) or different values on a given property.

MSSD and Comparable-Cases Control Strategies

In the comparative method matching as a control method plays a more important role than randomization. In the experimental and statistical methods randomization can be achieved more easily through manipulation and a large number of cases. When the number of cases is small randomization is more difficult. It means that cases are not enough to cover all the range of possible values on a given property or variable. The fact that matching is the main control technique in the comparative method has two main implications.

1. *Role of classification.* Because matching has such a central role in controlling unwanted sources of variation, in the comparative method conceptual treatment, classifications, and typologies become very important. The process of matching consists in *grouping cases according to similar values of given properties.* To keep constant a variable, all cases must have the same value on that variable. Thus, control through matching is gained by classifying and subclassifying (Smelser, 1976, pp. 168–169).

2. *"Most similar systems" design.* Consequently, for a number of authors comparative research designs are primarily designs in which cases are characterized by similarity. Lijphart (1975) argues "that it is more appropriate to reserve the term comparative method to the comparable-cases strategy and to assign the first solution [randomization] to the category of the statistical method" (p. 163). Cases are selected in such a way as to minimize the variance of control variables, and to maximize the variance of the experimental (independent and dependent) variables also to have a higher "degree of freedom."

Matching techniques were first developed in anthropology and introduced in sociology and political science as *methods of controlled comparisons* (Eggan, 1954; Hoenigswald, 1963), *specification* (Holt & Turner, 1970, p. 11) or *systematic comparative illustration* (Smelser, 1973, p. 53, 1976, p. 157). If researchers work with cases from a similar "area" with a homogeneous culture and similar socioeconomic conditions, they can control more factors than if they would draw their cases from very different cultural and socioeconomic contexts. For this reason, these authors are in favor of *middle-range theories*, that is, research designs that are limited in their generalizability but allow controlled explanations.

The method of "controlled comparisons" was imported in comparative political studies by the famous book by Przeworski and Teune (1970), *The Logic of Comparative Social Inquiry* (see also Meckstroth, 1975). This type of research design takes a number of labels, the two most frequently used being *"most similar systems" design* (Przeworski & Teune, 1970) and *comparable-cases strategy* (George, 1979; Lijphart, 1975). In MSSD, researchers compare two or more cases that are as similar as possible to be able to focus on variation of the independent and dependent variables that constitute the relationship of interest.[17]

MSSD is a research *design*. It refers to the choice of cases and variables. With MSSD researchers proceed in a similar way as in controlled comparisons. They select cases from a homogeneous context, which allows one to minimize the number of "experimental variables" while increasing number of "control variables." The more circumstances the selected cases have in common, the stronger the leverage to identify which factor accounts for the variation of the dependent variable. The drawback is that risks of diffusion effects increase (see Galton's problem above).

The Role of Classification

The table on the next page clarifies the double role of classification for both *comparability* and *control* by taking as an example the (s)election of heads of state.

First, classification is indispensable for establishing what is *comparable*. If we are interested in the election of heads of state we must exclude cases in which these are not elected. Germany, Italy, and Switzerland *do not share* the attribute "election of the head of state" (value 0) with France, the United States, Austria, and so on (values 1). In Germany, Italy, and Switzerland, the head of state is appointed by the parliament whereas in France, the United States, Austria, and so on, the head of state is elected by the people. Therefore, Germany, Italy, and Switzerland are not comparable with France, the United States, and Austria on this specific property. If the level of generality is higher, however, and we use a more abstract concept on the ladder of generality (*se*lection rather than *e*lection), then cases become comparable. In all the cases there is a selection of heads of state (value 1).

The noncomparable cases would be countries in which heads of state are not selected (value 0), such as constitutional monarchies in which the office of head of state is hereditary (Britain, Sweden, Spain, Netherlands, etc.).

Role of Classification	Level of Generality			
	Lower Level		Higher Level	
Comparability (same attribute)	Election (1) No election (0)		Selection (1) No selection (0)	
Matching (same value)	Direct: Austria, France, Portugal, Ireland, Finland	Indirect: United States	Election: Austria, France, Portugal, Ireland, Finland, United States	Appointment: Germany, Italy, Switzerland

Second, classification is indispensable for *matching* variables. To transform a variable into a constant we take cases with the same value. In the case of the election of head of states, this variable has two values: direct and indirect election. In the case of the selection of head of states, this variable has two values: election or appointment. Note that at the lower level of generality "election" is the shared *attribute*, at the higher level it is a *value* of the nominal variable "selection." If we wish to see the impact of party fragmentation on governmental stability we may want to "control for" the type of selection (election or appointment) as the legitimacy of a directly elected head of state may compensate for the party fragmentation. Classification allows the creation of groups of homogeneous cases.

CHAPTER 6. CAUSATION

Causes and Effects

This chapter deals with the *explanatory purposes* of the comparative method and the question of how to *accept or reject* hypotheses about causal relationships between variables, that is, how to *test* their empirical validity.

Methods of Inductive Inference

Causal relationships are the most interesting aspect of empirical research. Events do not just happen; they happen under certain conditions. Most research is about the *causes* of events or the *effects* of events. What are the causes of governmental instability? What are the factors that favor inflation? Does social security decrease work productivity? What is the effect of a change of electoral formula from proportional (PR) to majoritarian?

Although the term *cause* is very complex and controversial, it always involves a systematic association between events or phenomena. Events are uniformly connected. Causal statements imply lawlike regularities between cause and effect. The generality of causal connections is the assertion that a given phenomenon is invariably, or frequently, followed by another given phenomenon: no matter when and where.

The logical form of *conditional statements* about causal relationships is the following:

"if (*antecedent*) . . . , then (*consequent*) . . . "

In logical notation, the antecedent is usually symbolized as p and the consequent as q.

"if p . . . , then q . . . "

If the hypothesis is true, the antecedent implies the consequent. The *implication* is symbolized as $\supset$ or $\rightarrow$, which replace the verbal symbols "if . . . , then . . . :"

$$p \supset q \text{ or } p \rightarrow q$$

A conditional statement can be either *true* or *false* depending on whether p and q are present or absent in the real world. The truth of the implication of the conditional statement depends on the presence (1) or absence (0) of

p and q. Depending on the truth or not of the single components p and q of the conditional statement, the entire conditional statement is either true (1) or false (0). If, for example, we find a regular association between plurality electoral systems (present, or 1) and two-party systems (present, or 1), the conditional statement is true (1). If, on the contrary, we find cases with multiparty systems (two-party system is absent, or 0), then the conditional statement is false (0).

Establishing if conditional statements or hypotheses on causal relationships are true is a matter of *empirical* investigation. The truth of lawlike statements can only be established through the observation of reality. However, the observation of empirical experience is always limited to a reduced number of events: some cases, not all. Moving from observed facts concerning causal connections to universal statements is a matter of *inductive inference*. How can we infer general causal statements from observed instances?

The oldest type of inductive inference is *enumeration*. Evidence *in favor of* a conditional statement confirms it. There are two types of enumeration: (1) *inductive generalization* and (2) *analogy*. With inductive generalization, confirming instances of a causal connection are enumerated. For example, by listing countries with low-interest rates in which there has been an increase in prices, we may infer that "low-interest rates cause inflation;" or by listing countries with PR electoral systems in which there has been an increase of party systems' fragmentation we may infer that "PR causes party fragmentation." With analogy we infer on the *next* observation rather than a general law: we expect the next country that introduces PR to be also affected by fragmentation or the next economy to lower interest rates to have higher prices. Both types of enumeration are based on the same principle that the more the confirming instances, the higher the probability of the general causal connection.

Enumerative induction, however, is affected by a fundamental weakness: one single negative instance overthrows the law. Criticism toward enumerative inference and the argument by analogy as methods of inductive generalization was first formulated by Francis Bacon (1620), in *The New Organon*, who proposed other types of inductive procedures with the aim of replacing enumerative methods (until then based on Aristotle's logic). These were later refined by Mill (1843) and reformulated in *A System of Logic*. These procedures are known as Mill's methods of inductive inference. As will be seen later, the way in which these methods are used today is based on further elaborations, by Cohen and Nagel (1934), von Wright (1951), Popper (1959), and Hempel and Oppenheim (1948), stressing their eliminatory nature: conditional statements or hypotheses are accepted as true as long as they are not rejected or falsified.

Conditional Truth Table

On the basis of whether events are present (1) or absent (0) it is possible to construct a *truth table for conditional statements* in which the truth of the conditional statement is determined for all possible combinations (I to IV) making it possible to decide whether the hypothesis can be accepted or must be rejected. The column under the sign of the implication ($\rightarrow$) tells us if the conditional statement is either true (1) or false (0).

	p	$\rightarrow$	q
I	1	1	1
II	1	0	0
III	0	1	1
IV	0	1	0

The truth of the conditional statement ($\rightarrow$) is a function of the truth of p and q. The four possible combinations of p and q are (1, 1), (1, 0), (0, 1), and (0, 0). As it appears in the table, the conditional is always true (1) except for combination II. Eliminatory control processes are therefore based on this combination because it leads to the rejection of hypotheses.

Combination I means that if p is present (1) and q occurs (1), then the relationship is true. Combination II means that if p is present (1) but q does not occur (0), then the relationship does not exist. Combination III means that even if p is not present (0) q can still occur (1) because it can be caused by other factors (principle of the "plurality of the causes"). Combination IV means that the relationship exists if when p is not present (0) q does not occur (0).

Sufficient and Necessary Conditions

An important distinction that is relevant for Boolean methods is that between causes, or conditions under which events occur, that are either *necessary* or *sufficient* (Mackie, 1965; Mahoney, 2004).

A *sufficient condition* for the occurrence of an event q is a circumstance p in whose presence the event *always occurs*. If this type of condition is present, then q must occur. According to the truth table, when $p = 1$, $q = 1$ (combination I) and there is never a case of nonoccurrence ~q, that is, $p = 1$, $q = 0$ (combination II). However, the occurrence of q can also be produced by other causes (combination III): $p = 0$, $q = 1$.

Sufficient condition: p is a sufficient condition for q if q is always present when p occurs and q is never absent when p occurs. In Bayesian probability notation: $P(p \mid q) = 1$ and $P(p \mid {\sim}q) = 0$.

A *necessary condition* for the occurrence of an event q is a circumstance p in whose absence the event *cannot occur*. The event q occurs *only* if p is present, that is, when $q = 1$, $p = 1$ (combination I) and there is never a case of $\sim p$, that is, $p = 0$, $q = 1$ (combination III).

Necessary condition: p is a necessary condition for q if p is always present when q occurs and p is never absent when q occurs. In Bayesian probability notation: $P(p \mid q) = 1$ and $P({\sim}p \mid q) = 0$.

Conditional statements can be *reversed* or *converted*. If p is a *sufficient* condition for q, then q is a *necessary* condition for p. With the conditional statement $p \rightarrow q$, p is a sufficient condition for q, and q a necessary condition for p (if both p and q occur). Whenever p is present, q is present. In both cases this leads to $P(p \mid q) = 1$ (combination I). As Braumoeller and Goertz (2000) note, "any necessary condition hypothesis can be converted into a sufficient condition hypothesis and vice versa" (p. 846). If inequality is a sufficient condition for political instability, then political instability is a necessary condition for inequality. This, however, is confusing, since instability "comes after" inequality.

First, one must distinguish necessary *conditions* from necessary *causes*. Although all effects are necessary *conditions* of their sufficient causes, they are not always *causes*. Necessary causes are a subset of necessary conditions. A cause *"comes before"* (*temporally*) the effect. We must therefore distinguish (1) *"effective" necessary conditions* that establish the effect of a cause and (2) *"causal" necessary conditions* that establish the cause of an effect.

Second, one must distinguish *relevant* from *trivial* necessary conditions. The existence of a parliament is a necessary condition for a candidate to be elected, but is trivial and not useful for scientific advancement. Braumoeller and Goertz (2000) distinguish two steps in the methodology of necessary conditions. Step one establishes whether or not an event is a necessary condition (if not, step two becomes irrelevant). If necessary, step two establishes if an event is a relevant or trivial necessary condition (see section Trivialness in Chapter 7).

Summing up,

1. *Sufficient conditions:* If p is a sufficient condition for q, then p *implies* q, or q is implied by p, or $p \rightarrow q$ or $p \supset q$. Example: under

PR, receiving the most votes is a sufficient condition for being elected (but not necessary since second, third, etc. candidates also can be elected).

2. *Necessary conditions:* If p is a necessary condition for q, then p is *implied by* q, or q implies p, or $p \leftarrow q$ or $p \subset q$. Example: in two-ballot electoral systems, receiving the most votes in the first ballot is a necessary condition for being elected (but not a sufficient one since 50% are required at either the first or the second ballot).

3. *Sufficient and necessary conditions:* If p is a sufficient and necessary condition for q, then p implies and is implied by q and vice versa, or $p \equiv q$, or $p \leftrightarrow q$. This is called *equivalence* or *double conditional*. Example: under plurality, receiving the most votes is necessary and sufficient for being elected.

Mill's Methods

We start by discussing Mill's methods (and Przeworski and Teune's MSSD and MDSD) as both quantitative/statistical and qualitative/Boolean methods are based on them. Whereas the latter is based on Mill's first three "canons"—or methods of inductive inference (Skocpol, 1984a, p. 378; Zeldich, 1971, p. 267): (1) Method of Agreement, (2) Method of Difference, and (3) Joint Method of Agreement and Difference—the former is based on the Method of Concomitant Variations (even though, according to Mill, all methods ultimately are derived from the Method of Difference).

Method of Agreement

Mill defines the Method of Agreement as follows:

Method of Agreement (First Canon). "If two or more instances of the phenomenon under investigation have only one circumstance in common, the circumstance in which alone all the instances agree, is the cause (or effect) of the given phenomenon" (Mill, 1875, p. 451).

The researcher aims to explain a circumstance that is present in all the cases of interest (E). If these instances have only one of several possible antecedent circumstances in common (C), then this antecedent circumstance in which all the instances agree is the cause (or the effect) of the phenomenon.[18] This type of analysis can be represented in the following table where 1 symbolizes the presence of the circumstance and 0 its absence:

Instances (Cases)	Potential Causes (Independent Variables) C_1 C_2 C_3 C_4 C_5 . . . . . C_m										Phenomenon to Be Explained (Dependent Variable) E
1	0	1	1	1	1	.	.	.	.	.	1
2	1	0	1	0	1	.	.	.	.	.	1
3	1	0	0	1	1	.	.	.	.	.	1
4	1	1	0	0	1	.	.	.	.	.	1
5	1	1	0	1	1	.	.	.	.	.	1

Suppose there are five instances of social revolution (E) for which a researcher wishes to find the cause (C). Among the possible causes are unequal class structure (C_1), authoritarian political regime (C_2), weak international status (C_3), low levels of wealth (C_4), losing a war (C_5), and so on (C_m). All C_i that are not present in one or some of the five instances cannot be considered the cause of social revolutions. We may plausibly argue that poverty (C_4) is likely to provoke discontent among the population and revolutionary tendencies. However, if among the five cases the researcher finds cases in which the population is wealthy, then this factor must be excluded as a cause. Suppose further that the researcher rejects the candidate causes C_1, C_2, C_3 (besides C_4) as possible causes, but finds that in all five instances social revolutions there has been a defeat in a war before the revolution. Then the outcome of wars (C_5) is the cause of social revolutions according to the Method of Agreement.

The Method of Agreement is based on a causal connection between invariable antecedent and invariable consequent circumstances. As Ragin (1987, p. 37) notes, this method is in search for patterns of "invariance:" the constant circumstance in all instances of interest is explained by another (antecedent) circumstance, which is common among all instances.

The Method of Agreement is often associated with the MDSD (Przeworski & Teune, 1970, pp. 34–39) in which cases are drawn from different contexts where a large number of circumstances vary among instances. The researcher searches for commonalities between cases to identify the cause of the phenomenon of interest. In her book on *States and*

Social Revolutions, Skocpol (1979) explains three major cases in which revolutions occurred and stresses "crucial similarities" (Skocpol, 1984a, pp. 379–380) between cases that have very little in common: China, France, and Russia. The researcher controls for the effect (the consequent is invariably present) and—through the selection of cases from different contexts—is able to eliminate a large number of antecedent circumstances that are not commonly present among cases and, consequently, isolate the common circumstance(s).

Rightly, De Meur and Berg-Schlosser (1994) (see also note 16) stress that this design is really "Most Different with Similar Outcome" (MD-SO). They propose a *measure of the difference between cases* (say, countries) based on "Boolean distance" defined as the number of dichotomized variables by which pairs of cases differ (e.g., if two countries differ on many variables, they are more distant than if they differ in none). Through "(dis)similarity matrices" the authors select countries with similar outcomes (namely, breakdown of democracy after World War I) and identify where the crucial similarities explaining the same outcome lie.

What are the limitations of this method? First, this method suffers from the practical difficulties in fulfilling the requirement that the cases included in the sample vary according to all respects except one. Second, another limitation arises when two or more antecedent circumstances are found to be constant across instances. This method thus leaves open the question of which of the two or more constant antecedent circumstances is the actual cause of the phenomenon of interest. Finally, this method is unable to deal with multiple causation—E being caused by C_1 in one case and in C_3 in another.

Method of Difference

Mill defines the Method of Difference as follows:

Method of Difference (Second Canon). "If an instance in which the phenomenon under investigation occurs, and an instance in which it does not occur, have every circumstance in common save one, that one occurring only in the former; the circumstance in which alone the two instances differ, is the effect, or the cause, or an indispensable part of the cause, of the phenomenon" (Mill, 1875, p. 452).

Mill regarded the Method of Agreement as a weak demonstration of the causal association between phenomena and believed that its shortcomings could be overcome by the second method. If among all antecedent circumstances there is one that differs, than this is the cause or the effect of the phenomenon of interest. If C causes E, not only do we expect that C will be found when E is found, we also expect that if C does not occur, then E does not either. This method thus contrasts two types of instances: positive (1) and negative (0) outcomes E.

This method can be represented in the following table:

Instances (Cases)	Potential Causes (Independent Variables)							Phenomenon to Be Explained (Dependent Variable)
	C_1	C_2	C_3	C_4	C_5	. . . . . C_m		E
1	1	0	1	1	0	. . . . .		0
2	1	0	1	1	0	. . . . .		0
3	1	0	1	1	0	. . . . .		0
4	1	0	1	1	0	. . . . .		0
5	1	0	1	1	1	. . . . .		1

Michael Moore's movie *Bowling for Columbine* provides a good example. The difference he notices between the United States and other countries (Britain, Canada, France, Germany) is the much higher number of deaths by firearms in the United States. This difference cannot be explained through circumstances that are similar between these countries and Moore excludes such factors as violent past, ethnically mixed population, and poverty. A further excluded factor is the liberal sale of arms, insofar as this circumstance occurs in Canada as well. He concludes that the discriminant factor is the higher level of insecurity, which seems to pervade American society and is conveyed by a spectacularized commercial information system, and the lack of public welfare.

The Method of Difference considers instances similar in as many respects as possible. Similarity cannot account for difference. Factors that are common to all analyzed instances can therefore be excluded as causes. This method is often associated with the experimental method because it imitates "laboratory conditions" in which only one independent variable varies while other conditions are constant. Situations in which data approximate laboratory conditions are rare in the social sciences. Longitudinal data on a country at two different points in time provide such contexts (Skocpol, 1979, p. 37). Another way is to contrast empirical cases to imaginary or counterfactual cases such as ideal types (Bailey, 1982; Bonnell, 1980; Ragin, 1987, p. 39; Stinchcombe, 1978).

The Method of Difference is often associated with the MSSD (Przeworski & Teune, 1970, pp. 32–34). By choosing cases that have many properties in common the researcher can exclude them and concentrate on few properties that vary between cases and so test causal connections between them. This research design is typical of "area studies" in which cases are drawn from geographical regions of the world with a high number of common characteristics.

Here again De Meur and Berg-Schlosser (1994) stress that this design is "Most Similar with Different Outcome" (MS-DO) and through (dis)similarity matrices are able to identify cases with similar values for a small/large number of variables. Measuring the "Boolean distance" between pairs of cases allows one to isolate differences between cases that may explain the different outcome (in their example, the survival vs. breakdown of democratic regimes after World War I) among otherwise similar cases. For example, Finland and Estonia are by far the two closest cases. The "Boolean distance" is very small as the two countries have similar values for a high number of variables (only 14 out of 61 differ). Nonetheless, in one case democracy survived (Finland) whereas in the other it collapsed (Estonia). Tables of (dis)similarity allow one to direct research to those areas in which the most significant differences (that may explain the different outcome) are located. In the authors' example the different outcome between Finland and Estonia seems to be caused by different political cultures.

What De Meur and Berg-Schlosser have also emphasized is that—given the high number of potential variables that may account for an outcome in the social world—it is impossible to stick to the strict idea that there is "one decisive difference" (in the case of the Method of Difference) or "one decisive similarity" (in the case of the Method of Agreement). It seems obvious that the idea of looking for "the" *single* decisive similarity or difference is a rather flawed research strategy. Social reality is too complex for there to be a single cause of a given phenomenon that social scientists would be interested in. And, indeed, there are not many comparative analyses focused on isolating one (single) cause of a phenomenon.

First, the idea of one single factor accounting for the outcome must be interpreted in a verificatory manner, that is, through the formulation of specific hypotheses about their impact (see section Hypotheses and Deductive Validity below). Second, rather than testing for single factors, the comparative method tests the impact of combinations of factors (the combination of values or scores of two or more variables). For example, the presence of X_1 combined with the absence of X_2 account for a given outcome (see section on Multivariate Analysis with Logical Algebra). Third, to increase control the two methods (MD-SO and MS-DO) should be used jointly. As stressed above, the Method of Agreement on its own is unable to account for multiple causation (or "equifinality"), that is, the idea that there can be more than one cause for a same outcome. Only by complementing the MS-DO method with the MD-SO method, can multiple causation and causal complexity more generally be detected (see also section Disjunctions and Multiple Causation in Chapter 7). The need for combining the two methods leads us to talk about the main method used in social science comparisons.

Joint Method of Agreement and Difference (or Indirect Method)

The Joint Method is a combination of the two previous ones. Mill defines it as follows:

> *Joint Method of Agreement and Difference* (Third Canon). "If two or more instances in which the phenomenon occurs have only one circumstance in common, while two or more instances in which it does not occur have nothing in common save the absence of that circumstance; the circumstance in which alone the two sets of instances differ, is the effect, or the cause, or an indispensable part of the cause, of the phenomenon" (Mill, 1875, p. 458).

As seen above, a limitation of the Method of Agreement arises through cases in which two or more antecedent circumstances are found to be constant across instances. How is it possible to discriminate between them and decide which is the cause? The Method of Agreement offers no solution. The only solution is to introduce "negative cases" in which the outcome does not occur.

This method can be represented in the following table:

Instances (Cases)	Potential Causes (Independent Variables)										Phenomenon to Be Explained (Dependent Variable)
	C_1	C_2	C_3	C_4	C_5	.	.	.	.	C_m	E
1	1	1	1	1	1	.	.	.	.	.	1
2	1	0	1	0	1	.	.	.	.	.	1
3	1	0	0	1	1	.	.	.	.	.	1
4	1	1	0	0	1	.	.	.	.	.	1
5	1	1	0	1	1	.	.	.	.	.	1
6	1	0	1	0	0	.	.	.	.	.	0
7	1	1	1	0	0	.	.	.	.	.	0

Taking up the example used earlier, suppose that all five countries have a similar class structure (C_1) but have differences in political regimes, international status, and wealth. In such a case, the Method of Agreement would have eliminated C_2, C_3, and C_4, but left open the question of whether the class structure (C_1) or the outcome of wars (C_5) is the cause of revolutions. By taking only the five "positive cases," that is, where the outcome occurs $(E = 1)$, the Method of Agreement alone would not help us to discriminate. By adding the two negative cases 6 and 7 $(E = 0)$, the table shows that it is indeed C_5 that is the cause because the absence of C_5 is associated with the absence of E, whereas this is not true for C_1.

An example of the application of this method is Moore's (1966) *Social Origins of Dictatorship and Democracy* in which the author seeks to explain how different regimes developed. Using five main cases—England, France, United States, Japan, and China (and, less systematically, Prussia, Russia, and India)—Moore shows the impact of different class configurations. The alliance between bourgeoisie and aristocracy led to liberal democracy (England). Where the monarchy allied with aristocracy against the bourgeoisie the result was fascism (Japan). Where rural masses prevailed, the result was communism (China). Although the method is implicit in Moore's book, it remains one of the best examples of this kind of comparison.

By contrast, in her *States and Social Revolutions,* Theda Skocpol (1979) makes an explicit use of the Joint Method. Through the Method of Agreement she looks for common elements that may explain a similar outcome in three otherwise very different cases: France (1789), Russia (1917), and China (1947). She then introduces the Method of Difference with "negative" cases—in which social unrest did not produce a revolution: Prussia (1814), Germany (1848), and Japan (1868). This use of the Joint Method allows her to identify "state collapse" as the crucial variable. This factor is systematically present when revolutions occur, but absent when revolutions are absent. In all cases of revolution the state had previously been weakened by a great war that unraveled institutions and their capacity to respond to turmoil.

The Joint Method is, with some degree of confusion, often called the *Indirect Method of Difference.* The main reason why this alternative label is used is that the Method of Difference is really possible in laboratory conditions only, where the values or scores of variables can be manipulated. On the contrary, in the social sciences the variation of values or scores of a variable is obtained by considering both positive and negative cases—that is, cases in which the outcome is either present or absent.

Method of Concomitant Variations

With the Method of Concomitant Variations we leave the realm of "quality" (presence or absence of attributes) and enter the realm of "quantity" (variation in the magnitude or size of attributes). Rather than on dichotomous variables (0/1) this method is based on degrees and continuous variables.

Mill defines the Method of Concomitant Variations as follows:

> *Method of Concomitant Variations* (Fifth Canon). "Whatever phenomenon varies in any manner whenever another phenomenon varies in some particular manner, is either a cause or an effect of that phenomenon, or is connected with it through some fact of causation" (Mill, 1875, p. 464).

Conditional statements are formulated as covariations between the values of two or more variables: "the higher . . . , the higher . . . ," "the lower . . . , the lower . . . ," "the higher . . . , the lower . . . ," or finally "the lower . . . , the higher . . . ." For example, "older people (the higher age), tend to vote more conservative (say, measured on a left–right scale from 1 to 100)."

Ragin and Zaret (1983) contrast the Method of Concomitant Variations to Mill's first three methods by associating the former to the "*Durkheimian*" *quantitative-statistical* research strategy and the latter to the "*Weberian*" *comparative-qualitative* strategy. However, beside the fact that it is difficult to force all "comparativists" into a single Weberian camp (Skocpol, 1984a, p. 360), the Method of Agreement and the Method of Difference too are based on the association (covariation) between the presence or absence of an attribute (in the independent variable) and the presence or absence of another attribute (in the dependent variable). For this reason, the Method of Concomitant Variations, as all methods, ultimately relies on the Method of Difference for which one looks for associations between 0s and 1s. What differentiates the two methods is the discrete versus continuous nature of data.

Criticism of Mill's Methods

There are two main types of criticism against these methods, both directed against the claims that Mill (and Bacon before him) made about the importance of the methods as (1) devices for *discovering* the causes and the effects of phenomena and (2) logical tools for *demonstrating* the existence of cause–effect connections. The "claim" is that the methods would guide scientific research toward the discovery and proof of causal connections in a mechanical and systematic way (Cohen & Nagel, 1934, pp. 245–267; Copi, 1978, pp. 352–364).

1. *Methods for discovery.* First, Mill's methods require that all antecedent circumstances are included in the analysis in order to be able to identify causes. However, the inclusion of all circumstances (e.g., in the Method of Difference two instances must have *every* circumstance in common *save one*) would be, at best, cumbersome. The number of such circumstances is unlimited. For this reason, the requirement to include all antecedent factors must be interpreted as concerning only *relevant* factors.

The decision about the relevance of antecedent factors is not a matter of method but one of additional knowledge. The inclusion of antecedent factors in the "model" is a decision to be made *prior* to Mill's methods and is not guided by them. These methods do not eliminate the risk of ignoring relevant factors. They are therefore not methods for discovery of the unknown or unsuspected cause of an event. They are useful to identify the most likely cause among those factors that researchers "guessed" could potentially be of some relevance. That is to say that discovery is guided by theory.

Second, Mill's methods do not provide guidance for the analysis of antecedent circumstances. This is a matter of how the researcher treats potential explanatory variables. To reduce the number of variables one may group together explanatory factors (as, say, "culture") and find that a given political culture increases "social cohesion." One may, however, also consider several dimensions of political culture separately (levels of trust, type of identity, balance between tradition and modernity, etc.) and find out that only few influence political instability. Again, the analysis of antecedent circumstances can take place only in the light of additional knowledge prior to the use of Mill's methods.

2. *Methods for proof.* Concerning the claim that the methods are demonstrative, again there are two types of criticism. First, it follows from point 1 that if relevant factors are ignored and/or the analysis of antecedent circumstances is incorrect, the conclusion about the causal connections may be mistaken. From the impossibility to consider every possible antecedent circumstance—possibly combined with their incorrect analysis—follows also the impossibility to prove that one cause is really the cause. Relationships may be spurious, conditional, or indirect (Ragin, 1987, p. 37; Zelditch, 1971, pp. 300–305).

Second, and more generally, *inductive inferences* are never logically demonstrative (valid) since they are based on empirical observation confined to some—not all—instances. As long as there are unobserved cases, there is the possibility of evidence against the causal connection.

This criticism, however, applies not only to Mill's first three methods but equally to the Method of Concomitant Variation and statistics. Even in research designs relying upon a high number of observed cases, the inference to the properties of the still unobserved cases is never certain and is, at best, highly probable (see section Probabilistic Relationships in Chapter 8). In general, whereas valid *deductive* statements constitute proofs, *inductive* statements about causal connections are only probable.

The "discovery and proof" of causal connections thus requires *assumptions* concerning antecedent circumstances *before* employing the methods. On their own, Mill's methods are neither "sufficient" (Zelditch, 1971, p. 269) instruments of discovery nor proof.

Hypotheses and Deductive Validity

What, then, is the value of these methods if they are "neither methods of proof nor methods of discovery" (Cohen & Nagel, 1934, p. 266)? The claims above have been interpreted in a strict sense, but Mill himself meant to use his methods more modestly as a guide for systematic scientific exploration. So, although they are neither methods for discovery nor proof, they remain indispensable tools of analysis.

First, since it is impossible to include all antecedent circumstances, these methods require a prior formulation of *hypotheses*, that is, statements about circumstances researchers assume as relevant in explaining the observed event. The methods can thus only be used in conjunction with the formulation of hypotheses.

Second, these methods are rules for *eliminating false causal factors*. They are to be regarded as essentially *eliminative*, rather than enumerative inductive methods. A hypothesis is confirmed not because instances support it, but because it has not been rejected. Universal statements can never be verified; they can only be falsified (Popper, 1959, 1989). The elimination of hypotheses (*pars distruens*) leads to confirmation of hypotheses that resist falsification (*pars construens*). Eliminative induction provides a stronger inference. Evidence supporting a hypothesis can only be partial (never definite); its *rejection or elimination* is absolute (once for all). It is therefore important that hypotheses are formulated in a way to be falsifiable, through statements specifying the circumstances, which would prove their falsity.

If one defines a set of alternative hypotheses concerning the causes of E (with C_1, C_2, C_3, or C_4 as hypothetical explanatory factors) and eliminates the C_1, C_2, and C_4 factors as possible causes of E but not C_3, it follows that C_3 is confirmed as the cause of E. Not only has the hypothesis concerning the causal connection between C_3 and E not been rejected (inductively) through the test against evidence (whereas C_1, C_2, and C_4 have been rejected), but in addition the inference is based on a *valid deductive argument* (*modus tollens*) with the following syllogism (in this example it is applied to the Method of Agreement):

If C_1 is the cause of E, then E cannot occur in the absence of C_1
There is one (or more than one) instance in which E occurs in the absence of C_1

∴ C_1 is not the cause of E

The conclusion is deductively valid because the argument includes a *hypothesis* (or, more precisely, a "hypothetical premise") in the first line of the syllogism. Consequently, Cohen and Nagel (1934) have proposed a "negative formulation" of the Methods of Agreement and Difference in line with the eliminatory epistemology of hypothesis testing. According to this formulation, the first two canons read as follows:

Method of Agreement: "Nothing can be the cause of a phenomenon which is not a common circumstance in all the instances of the phenomenon" (Cohen & Nagel, 1934, p. 255).

Method of Difference: "Nothing can be the cause of a phenomenon if the phenomenon does not take place when the supposed cause does" (Cohen & Nagel, 1934, p. 259).[19]

There must be a hypothesis H or a set of alternative hypotheses (H_1, H_2, H_3, . . .). Empirical research eliminates those which are not true. In the next section the distinction between sufficient and necessary conditions is reintroduced and strategies for establishing causal connections are presented. In doing this, we follow two strategies: (1) based on *effects* and (2) based on *causes*. With the former, researchers identify the causes of phenomena (mostly in social sciences). With the latter researchers identify the effects of phenomena (typical of laboratory research). The difference between the two research strategies lies in the selection of positive and negative cases.

CHAPTER 7. COMPARATIVE ANALYSIS
WITH BOOLEAN ALGEBRA

This chapter is divided into three main parts. First, the five methods for testing single factors as sufficient and/or necessary conditions are presented. These are based on the Methods of Agreement and Difference, and on the Joint Method (or Indirect Method). Second, combinatorial methods are introduced in which explanation is based on the configuration of the values of independent variables. Both these sections deal with dichotomous data, that is, variables that assume either a value of presence (1) or absence (0). Third, the methods are extended to nondichotomous data, namely to fuzzy-set analysis.

The Search for Sufficient Conditions

Based on Effects (Method 1)

As seen earlier, sufficient conditions are easier to interpret in terms of sufficient "causes" than necessary conditions. We therefore start with sufficient conditions. If C (a hypothetical cause) is a sufficient condition for E (a hypothetical effect), then C implies E and the conditional truth table looks as follows:

	C	$\rightarrow$	E
I	1	1	1
II	1	0	0
III	0	1	1
IV	0	1	0

with $C \rightarrow E$ (the 0/1 values in the cells never change).

If C is a sufficient condition for E, then there is never a case in which C is present and E is absent. That is to say, there is never the combination $C = 1$ and $E = 0$ (combination II) or in Bayesian probability notation $P(C \mid \sim E) = 0$. Note, therefore, that it is combination II that rejects the hypothesis. If, for example, PR electoral systems are a sufficient condition for multiparty systems, then there must never be a two-party system when PR exists.

According to the deductive argument:

If C is a sufficient condition for E, then C cannot occur in the absence of E
There is one (or more than one) instance in which C occurs in the absence of E

∴ C is not a sufficient condition for E

In practice, with this research strategy, *cases are selected such that all* $E = 0$. The potential sufficient conditions $(C_1, C_2, C_3, \ldots)$ are then examined and, possibly, excluded. According to combination II of the truth table, we eliminate the combinations $C = 1$, $E = 0$.

Instances (Cases)	Potential Sufficient Conditions (Independent Variables) C_1 C_2 C_3 C_4 C_5 . . . . C_m	Effect (Dependent Variable) E
1	1 0 1 1 0	0
2	0 0 1 1 0	0
3	0 0 1 1 0	0
4	1 0 0 1 0	0
5	1 0 0 1 1	0

According to this table, we exclude as sufficient causes all potential conditions with the exception of C_2. That is to say, we do not reject cases in which $C = 0$, $E = 0$ (combination IV).

Based on Causes (Method 2)

If C is a sufficient condition for E, every time that C is present E must also occur. If E is not present, then C is not a sufficient condition for E. Again, C implies E ($C \rightarrow E$) and the conditional truth table is the same as for Method 1 above.

As for methods based on effects, if C is a sufficient condition for E, then there is never a case in which C is present and E is absent. That is to say, that there is never the combination $C = 1$ and $E = 0$ (combination II) or in Bayesian probability notation $P(C \mid {\sim}E) = 0$. Note, again, that it is combination II that rejects the hypothesis.

The deductive argument too remains the same:

If C is a sufficient condition for E, then C cannot occur in the absence of E
There is one (or more than one) instance in which C occurs in the absence of E

∴ C is not a sufficient condition for E

In practice, however, the research strategy is different. Rather than selecting cases in which $E = 0$, that is, negative cases in which the effect does not occur, we select cases according to the value $C = 1$, that is, all cases in which the condition we hypothesize as sufficient is present. According to this method, *cases are selected such that all $C = 1$*. The effects $(E_1, E_2, E_3, \dots)$ are then examined and, possibly, alternative hypotheses are excluded. According to combination II of the truth table, we eliminate the combinations $C = 1$, $E = 0$.

Instances (Cases)	Potential Sufficient Condition (Independent Variable) C_1	Effects (Dependent Variables) E_1	E_2	E_3	E_4	.	.	.	E_m
1	1	0	1	1	0	.	.	.	.
2	1	0	1	1	0	.	.	.	.
3	1	0	1	1	0	.	.	.	.
4	1	0	0	1	1	.	.	.	.
5	1	0	0	1	0	.	.	.	.

This is a more "experimental" and practice-oriented approach in which one controls the causes and tries to identify what their effects are. According to this table, we exclude C as a sufficient condition for E_1, E_2, and E_4. We do not exclude C as a sufficient condition of E_3. That is to say, we do not reject cases in which $C = 1$, $E = 1$ (combination I).

The Search for Necessary Conditions

Based on Effects (Method 3)

With this method, given an event E, we want to know which factors, among a number of potential alternative necessary conditions, are to be rejected and which not. As seen above, if C (a hypothetical cause) is a necessary condition for E (a hypothetical effect), then C is implied by E ($C \leftarrow E$) and the conditional truth table looks as follows:

	E	$\rightarrow$	C
I	1	1	1
II	1	0	0
III	0	1	1
IV	0	1	0

with $E \rightarrow C$ rather than $C \rightarrow E$ (as for sufficient conditions).

If C is a necessary condition for E, then there is never a case in which C is absent and E is present. That is to say that there is never the combination $C = 0$ and $E = 1$ (combination II) or in Bayesian probability notation $P(\sim C \mid E) = 0$. It is again combination II that rejects the hypothesis. If a civic political culture is a necessary condition for the stability of democracies, then there is never a case in which a civic political culture is absent and democracy is stable.

According to the deductive argument:

If C is a necessary condition for E, then C cannot be absent in the presence of E
There is one (or more than one) instance in which C is absent in the presence of E

$\therefore$ C is not a necessary condition for E

In practice, with this research strategy, *cases are selected such that all $E = 1$.* The potential necessary conditions ($C_1, C_2, C_3, \ldots$) are then examined and, possibly, excluded. According to combination II of the truth table, we eliminate combinations in which $C = 0, E = 1$.

Instances (Cases)	Potential Necessary Conditions (Independent Variable)									Effect (Dependent Variables)
	C_1	C_2	C_3	C_4	C_5	.	.	.	C_m	E
1	1	0	1	1	0	.	.	.		1
2	0	0	1	1	0	.	.	.		1
3	0	0	1	1	0	.	.	.		1
4	1	0	0	1	0	.	.	.		1
5	1	0	0	1	1	.	.	.		1

According to this table, we exclude as necessary conditions for E all potential conditions with the exception of C_4. That is to say, we do not reject cases in which $C = 1$, $E = 1$ (combination I).

As Braumoeller and Goertz (2000, p. 846) note, when testing the proposition that C is a necessary condition for E if C is always present when E occurs, cases in which $E = 0$ are irrelevant. This appears in the following table:

In this table, C is always present when E is present: $P(C \mid E) = 1$. We thus select only cases in which $E = 1$.

Based on Causes (Method 4)

If C is a necessary condition for E, every time that C is absent E cannot occur. If E is present, then C is not a necessary condition for E. Again, C implies E ($C \rightarrow E$) and the conditional truth table is the same as above in Method 3 based on effects.

As for methods based on effects, if C is a necessary condition for E, then there is never a case in which C is absent and E is present. That is to say, that there is never the combination $C = 0$ and $E = 1$ (combination II) or in Bayesian probability notation $P(\sim C \mid E) = 0$. It is always combination II that rejects the hypothesis.

The deductive argument too remains the same:

If C is a necessary condition for E, then C cannot be absent in the presence of E
There is one (or more than one) instance in which C is absent in the presence of E

∴ C is not a necessary condition for E

In practice, however, the research strategy is different. Rather than selecting cases in which $E = 1$, that is, positive cases in which the effect occurs, we select cases according to the value $C = 0$, that is, all cases in which the condition we hypothesize as necessary is absent. With this research strategy *cases are selected such that all $C = 0$*. The effects (E_1, E_2, E_3, ...) are then examined and, possibly, alternative hypotheses are excluded. According to combination II of the truth table, we eliminate combinations in which $C = 0$, $E = 1$.

Instances (Cases)	Potential Necessary Condition (Dependent Variable) C_1	Effects (Independent Variables)						
		E_1	E_2	E_3	E_4	.	. .	E_m
1	0	1	1	0	0	.	. .	.
2	0	1	1	0	0	.	. .	.
3	0	0	1	0	0	.	. .	.
4	0	0	0	0	1	.	. .	.
5	0	0	0	0	1	.	. .	.

Again, being a method based on causes, this is a more "experimental" approach. According to this table, we exclude C as a necessary condition for E_1, E_2, and E_4. We do not exclude C as a necessary condition of E_3. We do not reject cases in which $C = 0$, $E = 0$ (combination IV). Testing the proposition that C is a necessary condition for E if E does not occur in the absence of C, cases in which $C = 1$ are irrelevant. This appears in the following table:

C is never present when E does not occur: $P(\sim C \mid \sim E) = 1$. We select only cases in which $C = 0$.

In sum, in all four methods we reject H according to combination II $(0,1)$. With the methods based on causes we do not reject H based on combination IV $(0,0)$ and with the methods based on effects we do not reject H based on combination I $(1,1)$.

These four methods are instruments for rejecting false hypotheses to be used with different research strategies. If we want to test if a PR electoral system is a *sufficient condition* for multiparty systems (MPS) we can (1) based on *causes* select cases in which PR = 1 and see if in all MPS = 1, and (2) based on *effects* select cases in which MPS = 0 (two-party systems) and see if there are cases in which PR = 1. Conversely, if we want to test if a PR electoral system is a *necessary condition* for MPS we can (1) based on *causes* select cases of majoritarian systems (PR = 0) and see if there is MPS and (2) based on *effects* select cases in which MPS = 1 and see if there are cases in which PR = 0.

In conclusion, the control of hypotheses can be done in various ways: select causes and observe their effects or select effects and track their

62

causes. The choice of a research strategy often depends on which and how many cases are available. In practice, the combination of diverse methods always strengthens results.

"Trivialness"

Braumoeller and Goertz are the first to formalize "trivialness." They illustrate the point by asking "what makes gravity trivially necessary for war?" (2000, p. 854) (see also Goertz & Starr, 2003). There are two main forms of trivialness and one case of nontrivialness:

1. *Trivial Type 1* (left-hand table). C is a necessary condition for E if C is always present when E occurs. If we select cases with $E = 1$, there must always be $C = 1$ (*Method 3*). However, C may be present even when $E = 0$. Is gravity a necessary condition for war? Yes, because gravity is always present ($C = 1$) when there is a war ($E = 1$), however it is also present when there is no war ($E = 0$). In this case there is no variation in the *independent* variable (C). Gravity is a trivial necessary condition for wars when it is present in both cases of war and nonwar:

$$P(C \mid {\sim}E) = 1 \text{ and } P(C \mid E) = 1$$

2. *Trivial Type 2* (center table). C is a necessary condition for E if E does not occur in the absence of C. If we select cases with $C = 0$, there must always be $E = 0$ (*Method 4*). However, E may be absent even when $C = 1$. Is the presence of at least one authoritarian state a necessary condition for war? Yes, because war is always absent ($E = 0$) when there are no authoritarian states ($C = 0$). However, E is also absent when there are authoritarian states. In this case there is no variation in the *dependent* variable (E). Authoritarian states are a trivial necessary condition for wars when there are no wars:

$$P({\sim}C \mid {\sim}E) = 1 \text{ and } P(C \mid {\sim}E) = 1$$

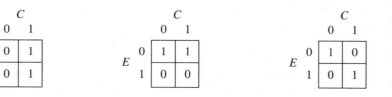

| | | *Trivial Type 1* | | | | *Trivial Type 2* | | | | *Nontrivial* | |

		C				C				C	
		0	1			0	1			0	1
E	0	0	1	E	0	1	1	E	0	1	0
	1	0	1		1	0	0		1	0	1

3. *Nontrivial* (right-hand table). To avoid Types 1 and 2 of trivialness there must be variation in both the *independent and dependent* variables (*C* and *E*). To avoid Trivial Type 1 we need a variation in the independent variable (*C*). To avoid Trivial Type 2 we need a variation in the dependent variable (*E*). In practice, this means that we need to use both *Methods 3* and *4* to assess for nontrivial necessary conditions. If PR is a necessary condition for MPS, PR is always present when MPS occur: $P(C \mid E) = 1$. However, to be nontrivial (Type 1), it must not be present when MPS are absent: $P(C \mid \sim E) = 0$ (rather than $=1$). In addition, if PR is a necessary condition for MPS, MPS does not occur in the absence of PR: $P(\sim C \mid \sim E) = 1$. However, to be nontrivial (Type 2), PR must not occur when there are no MPS: $P(C \mid \sim E) = 0$ (rather than $=1$). In sum:

$$P(C \mid E) = 1 \text{ and } P(\sim C \mid \sim E) = 1$$

Sufficient and Necessary Conditions (Method 5)

The four methods discussed above provide the basis for more complex analyses. First, they allow identification of conditions that are both sufficient and necessary (this section). Second, they provide the tools for multivariate analysis and compound statements (next section).

To identify conditions that are both sufficient and necessary one uses two truth tables. The combination of the truth table for sufficient conditions with the truth table for necessary conditions allows one to identify conditions that are both sufficient *and* necessary. However, instead of rejecting hypotheses uniquely on the basis of combination II, the combinations leading to the rejection of a hypothesis are two: combinations II and III.

The truth table looks as follows

	C	$\leftrightarrow$	*E*
I	1	1	1
II	1	0	0
III	0	0	1
IV	0	1	0

with $\leftrightarrow$ (or $\equiv$) symbolizing the *equivalence* or "*double*" *implication*. The difference with "simple" implication is that both combinations II and III have a 0 in the central column rather than combination II only.

In practice, the two truth tables are used subsequently. First, one eliminates conditions that are not sufficient. Second, among those that "survived" the first phase, one eliminates conditions that are not necessary. The remaining condition(s) are both sufficient *and* necessary.

Instances (Cases)	Potential Sufficient and Necessary Conditions (Independent Variables)								Effect (Dependent Variable)
	C_1	C_2	C_3	C_4	C_5	. . . .	C_m		E
1	1	1	1	1	1	. . . .			1
2	1	0	1	0	1	. . . .			1
3	1	0	0	1	1	. . . .			1
4	1	1	0	0	1	. . . .			1
5	1	1	0	1	1	. . . .			1
6	1	0	1	0	0	. . . .			0
7	1	1	1	0	0	. . . .			0

If C is a sufficient condition for E, then when C is present E is always present too: $P(C \mid E) = 1$; and when C is present E can never be absent: $P(C \mid {\sim}E) = 0$. Otherwise we reject H on the basis of combination II. In the table above this eliminates C_1, C_2, and C_3 as sufficient conditions for E. Furthermore, if C is a necessary condition for E, then when E is present, C must be present too: $P(C \mid E) = 1$; and when E is present C can never be absent: $P({\sim}C \mid E) = 0$. Otherwise we reject H on the basis of combination III. This eliminates C_4 as a necessary condition for E. C_5 is the only sufficient and necessary condition in this example. This method is based on the Joint Method of Agreement and Difference (or Indirect Method).

Multivariate Analysis With Logical Algebra

The previous methods have sometimes been criticized for being complex and cumbersome in particular when applied to multivariate analysis.

Improvements came from the further development of logical calculus (Cohen & Nagel, 1934; Nagel, Suppes, & Tarski, 1963; Roth, 2004; von Wright, 1951). First, this section presents the basic operators of logical algebra and illustrates their use in multivariate research designs. Second, Boolean analysis is introduced. Recent influential contributions have stressed the possibilities set algebra offers for the study of multivariate relationships (Ragin, 1987, pp. 85–163). The possibility of taking into account explanatory variables as configurations or combinations is one of the main strengths of modern comparative research designs.

Compound Statements

In multivariate analysis researchers look for sufficient and/or necessary conditions in the form of *compound attributes* rather than simple attributes, that is, "packages" of attributes. Ragin has made this "combinatorial logic" the distinctive feature of the comparative method (Ragin, 1987, p. 15). Rather than testing the empirical validity of hypotheses concerning potential sufficient or necessary conditions one by one or in an additive logic, conditions are tested when they combine in specific ways. To understand how this works, a few basic elements of logical algebra must be introduced.

Multivariate analysis is based on three fundamental Boolean *operators* or *connectives* for compound statements: AND, OR, and NOT.

1. The *conjunction* (AND) symbolized as · (or $\wedge$). The conjunction produces a compound statement in which both components (C_1 and C_2) are true (present). Whenever either component (or both) is false (0), the conjunction is false. The truth table shows the value of a compound statement for all combinations of values for its components:

C_1	C_2	$C_1 \cdot C_2$
1	1	1
1	0	0
0	1	0
0	0	0

2. The (inclusive) *disjunction* (OR) symbolized as + (or $\vee$).[20] The disjunction produces a compound statement in which either (or both) its components is true. It is false only when both of them are false.

The truth table shows the value of a compound statement for every possible combination of values for its components:

C_1	C_2	$C_1 \vee C_2$
1	1	1
1	0	1
0	1	1
0	0	0

3. The *negation* (NOT) symbolized as ~. The negation produces a statement that reverses the truth value of any statement (simple or compound). It is particularly important as it represents the absence of a causal condition ($C = 0$) or outcome ($E = 0$).[21]

Take the following example of a *conjunction* (AND). We may find that the single attribute PR is not a sufficient condition for MPS to occur nor that the single attribute social fragmentation (SF) is a sufficient condition for MPS, but that the compound attribute "PR and SF" (PR · SF) is a sufficient condition to produce MPS. According to Method 2 we would eliminate both PR and SF singularly as sufficient conditions for MPS (in Case 4 PR does not produce a MPS and in Case 5 SF does not produce a MPS). However, the presence of both PR and SF is a sufficient condition for MPS.

Instances (Cases)	Potential Sufficient Conditions			Effect
	PR	SF	PR · SF	MPS
1	1	1	1	1
2	1	1	1	1
3	1	1	1	1
4	1	0	0	0
5	0	1	0	0

In Boolean algebra the conjunction AND is called *multiplication*. The product is a *specific combination of causal conditions*. The statement PR · SF → MPS is written as

$$MPS = PR \cdot SF \text{ (or, simply, } MPS = PR\ SF)$$

When PR and SF are both present, then MPS is also present. With this type of notation $1 \cdot 0 = 0$ or, conversely, $0 \cdot 1 = 0$. If only one of the two components is present, then the outcome does not occur. The presence of PR is combined with the presence of SF to produce MPS, whereas the absence of any of the two simple statements does not lead to the outcome. A compound statement of this sort can also include "absence" of properties. For example, it is only the combination of majoritarian electoral system (M), "no SF" (~SF), and "no territorially concentrated minorities" (~TCM) to produce a two-party system (TPS),

$$TPS = M \cdot \text{~SF} \cdot \text{~TCM} \ (\text{or } TPS = M \ sf \ tcm)$$

with *uppercase* letters indicating the presence of the attribute and *lowercase* letters indicating the absence (negation) of the attribute.

In Boolean algebra the *disjunction* OR is called *addition* and is symbolized through +. Here the addition consists of the fact that if any of the conditional components is present, then the outcome occurs. In this type of algebra therefore, $1 + 1 = 1$. If, for example, we ask what leads to a loss of votes for a party at a given election (LV), we may find evidence that various factors lead to the same outcome: a poor performance in government (PP), the emergence of a new concurrent party in the same ideological family (NP) or a political scandal involving the leader of the party (PS). If any one, or any two or all three factors are true, then the outcome LV occurs. The conditional statement PP ∨ NP ∨ PS → LV is written as

$$LV = PP + NP + PS$$

meaning that either a poor performance in government or a new concurrent party or a political scandal can each cause a loss of votes for the party (or all three or any two).

Compound statements based on conjunctions and disjunctions are crucial to distinguish: (1) sufficient but not necessary conditions, (2) necessary but not sufficient conditions, (3) neither sufficient nor necessary conditions, and (4) both sufficient and necessary conditions.

Disjunctions and Multiple Causation

1. *Sufficient but not necessary conditions.* Disjunctions or Boolean additions (OR) are particularly important because they allow to formalize *multiple (or plural) causation.* Evidence may sometimes show that a given

cause is not the *only* cause (Zelditch, 1971, p. 299). Disjunction or addition indicates that a causal condition can be replaced by another in producing the outcome.

Multiple causation can be expressed in the following way: a given condition C_1 is sufficient to produce the outcome E. However, since it is not the only possible cause, the same outcome E can be produced by another sufficient condition C_2. This is what the disjunction (Boolean addition [+]) signifies. The equation is:

$$E = C_1 + C_2$$

According to Method 2 based on causes to establish sufficient conditions, if C_1 is a sufficient condition, when $C_1 = 1$ we must always find $E = 1$, that is, $P(C_1 \mid E) = 1$ and never $E = 0$, that is, $P(C_1 \mid {\sim}E) = 0$. Similarly, if C_2 is a sufficient condition, when $C_2 = 1$ we must always find $E = 1$, that is, $P(C_2 \mid E) = 1$ and never $E = 0$, that is, $P(C_2 \mid {\sim}E) = 0$. If this is the case, both C_1 and C_2 are sufficient to produce E. However, neither is necessary as Cases 4 and 5 show (the outcome occurs when $C_1 = 0$ or $C_2 = 0$).

Cases	C_1	C_2	$C_1 + C_2$	E
1	1	1	1	1
2	1	1	1	1
3	1	1	1	1
4	1	0	1	1
5	0	1	1	1

Multiple causation represents disjunctive configurations (OR, +) in which C_1 and C_2 are *sufficient but not necessary* conditions.

Conjunctions and Combinatorial Causation

2. *Necessary but not sufficient conditions.* Conjunctions or Boolean multiplications (AND) are important because they allow to formalize *combinatorial causation*. Data may show that a given cause does not produce an effect on its own but only in conjunction with another. This

means that a causal condition must be accompanied by another to produce the outcome.

Combinatorial causation can be expressed in the following way: a given condition C_1 is necessary to lead to the outcome E. However, since it is not a sufficient condition, the outcome E can only be produced if accompanied by another sufficient condition C_2. This is what the conjunction (Boolean multiplication [·]) signifies. The equation is

$$E = C_1 \cdot C_2$$

According to Method 3 based on effects, if C_1 is a necessary condition for E, when $E = 1$ we must always find $C_1 = 1$, that is, $P(C_1 \mid E) = 1$ and never $C_1 = 0$, that is, $P(\sim C_1 \mid E) = 0$. Similarly, if C_2 is a necessary condition for E, when $E = 1$ we must always find $C_2 = 1$, that is, $P(C_2 \mid E) = 1$ and never $C_2 = 0$, that is, $P(\sim C_2 \mid E) = 0$. If this is the case, both C_1 and C_2 are necessary for E. However, none is sufficient on its own as Case 4 (for C_1) and Case 5 (for C_2) show.

Cases	C_1	C_2	$C_1 \cdot C_2$	E
1	1	1	1	1
2	1	1	1	1
3	1	1	1	1
4	1	0	0	0
5	0	1	0	0

Combinatorial causation represents conjunctive configurations (AND, ·) in which C_1 and C_2 are *necessary but not sufficient* conditions.

Combining Connectives

3. *Neither sufficient nor necessary conditions.* Let us take a more complicated example in which no condition is either sufficient nor necessary, but in which two combinations of conditions are both sufficient to produce the outcome E:

$$E = (C_1 \cdot C_2) + (C_3 \cdot \sim C_4)$$

If we take the four potential causal conditions separately, neither is sufficient nor necessary as it appears in the following table:

Cases	C_1	C_2	$C_1 \cdot C_2$	C_3	C_4	$C_3 \cdot \sim C_4$	E
1	1	1	1	1	0	1	1
2	1	1	1	1	0	1	1
3	1	1	1	1	0	1	1
4	0	1	0	0	0	0	1
5	1	0	0	1	0	1	1
6	0	1	0	0	1	0	0
7	1	0	0	1	1	0	0

First, it is easy to see that no condition is sufficient on its own to produce the outcome E because all C_i are present when E does not occur (in the last two rows: Cases 6 and 7) according to Method 2. Second, by selecting cases in which $E = 1$ (*Method 3*), that is, when the outcome occurs, it is possible to eliminate all four C_i as necessary conditions, as E also occurs when the potential causal conditions are absent (in Cases 4 and 5). Therefore, none of the four potential causal conditions are either sufficient or necessary for E.

However, the expression above indicates that the combination between C_1 and C_2 produces E or, alternatively, that the combination between C_3 and the absence of C_4 (when $C_4 = 0$) produces E. Both combinations $C_1 \cdot C_2$ and $C_3 \cdot \sim C_4$ are sufficient to produce the outcome: each time the first combination is present the outcome occurs and the same applies to the second combination. However, neither is necessary, as the outcome E occurs also when the two combinations do not occur (Cases 4 and 5).

4. *Necessary and sufficient conditions.* Finally, conjunctions and disjunctions can be used to interpret conditions that are both necessary and sufficient.

- A *sufficient* condition C_1 means that there is no need for it to be in conjunction (through the AND connective) with any other variable C_i to produce E. C_1 is one that by itself always produces the outcome: $P(C_1 \mid E) = 1$ and $P(C_1 \mid \sim E) = 0$.

- A *necessary* condition C_1 means that it cannot be replaced (through the disjunctive OR connective) by any other variable C_i to produce E. C_1 must always be present to produce the outcome: $P(C_1 \mid E) = 1$ and never $E = 0$, that is, $P(\sim C_1 \mid E) = 0$.

In Boolean terms,

$$E = C_1$$

representing the following table where C_1 is both sufficient and necessary:

Cases	C_1	E
1	1	1
2	1	1
3	1	1
4	1	1
5	1	1

Simplifying Data

As seen, compound statements are based on different combinations of the two connectives conjunction and disjunction ("sums-of-products"), as well as the negation. This allows complex but sometimes long statements. A number of logical devices are useful to simplify data.

1. *Minimization.* The first device for simplifying causal statements is minimization. This tool eliminates causal conditions that appear in one combination of factors (conjunction) but not (disjunction) in another combination of factors otherwise equal to the first one. If *only one* causal condition is different between two combinations of factors both producing the outcome E (say, C_3 is present in one while absent in the other), this causal condition can be considered irrelevant for the outcome.

Take three factors C_1, C_2, and C_3 whose simultaneous presence (through the connective AND) is sufficient to produce E. Imagine further that a second combination of factors (through the connective OR) is also sufficient to produce E. In the second combination, however, C_3 is absent ($\sim C_3$). We have the following compound statement:

$$E = (C_1 \cdot C_2 \cdot C_3) + (C_1 \cdot C_2 \cdot \sim C_3)$$

These are two alternative combinations of factors both sufficient to produce E. None of the single factors C_i are sufficient (see Cases 4 to 6) nor are they necessary (see Cases 7 to 9) on their own for E. However, the two combinations are sufficient conditions (but not necessary). In the first combination three C_i factors are present. Therefore, $C_1 \cdot C_2 \cdot C_3 = 1$. In the second combination the first two C_i are present but C_3 is absent. Thus, $C_1 \cdot C_2 \cdot \sim C_3 = 1$.

Cases	C_1	C_2	C_3	$C_1 \cdot C_2 \cdot C_3$	C_1	C_2	C_3	$C_1 \cdot C_2 \cdot \sim C_3$	E
1	1	1	1	1	1	1	0	1	1
2	1	1	1	1	1	1	0	1	1
3	1	1	1	1	1	1	0	1	1
4	0	1	1	0	0	1	1	0	0
5	1	0	1	0	1	0	1	0	0
6	1	1	0	0	1	1	0	0	0
7	0	1	1	0	0	1	1	0	1
8	1	0	1	0	1	0	1	0	1
9	1	1	0	0	1	1	0	0	1

It is clear that the presence or absence of C_3 is not influential in producing the outcome E and therefore can be eliminated. Whether or not C_3 is present, E occurs anyway. The "*primitive*" *statement* can be simplified into the following "*minimized*" *statement*:

$$E = C_1 \cdot C_2$$

The combination $C_1 \cdot C_2$ is a sufficient condition for E.

The logic on which minimization is based is eminently an experimental one in which between two combinations of factors both producing the same outcome E, *there is only one varying factor* (present in one combination and absent in the other). According to the Method of Difference in an MSSD framework, the only factor that varies while the outcome is constant and all other factors are constant, this can be eliminated as a causal factor.

2. *Implication.* The second device for simplifying causal statements is the implication or the use of "prime implicants." Prime implicants are minimized statements that cover more than one primitive statement. In the example above, the minimized prime implicant $(C_1 \cdot C_2)$ covers both $(C_1 \cdot C_2 \cdot C_3)$ and $(C_1 \cdot C_2 \cdot \sim C_3)$. It is said to imply, cover, or include them. Primitive statements are *subsets* of the prime implicant. Both $(C_1 \cdot C_2 \cdot C_3)$ and $(C_1 \cdot C_2 \cdot \sim C_3)$ are a subset of $(C_1 \cdot C_2)$. The membership of both $(C_1 \cdot C_2 \cdot C_3)$ and $(C_1 \cdot C_2 \cdot \sim C_3)$ is included in the membership of $(C_1 \cdot C_2)$.

In some cases, *several* prime implicants cover the *same* primitive statements. Prime implicants themselves are therefore redundant and minimized statements can be further simplified. This leads to a maximum of parsimony in which only essential prime implicants appear in the causal statement.

Take four cases in which E occurs and we wish to establish which of three potential causal conditions are sufficient and/or necessary. In the following table one sees that there are four alternative combinations (AND) of the C_i producing the outcome E linked through a disjunction OR since all are alternative sufficient conditions for E:

Cases	C_1	C_2	C_3	E
1	1	0	1	1
2	0	1	0	1
3	1	1	0	1
4	1	1	1	1

The primitive statement for this table is the following, where each product corresponds to a row (case) in the previous table:

$$E = (C_1 \cdot \sim C_2 \cdot C_3) + (\sim C_1 \cdot C_2 \cdot \sim C_3) + (C_1 \cdot C_2 \cdot \sim C_3) + (C_1 \cdot C_2 \cdot C_3)$$

According to the minimization principle discussed above

Cases	1 4	$(C_1 \cdot \sim C_2 \cdot C_3)$ $(C_1 \cdot C_2 \cdot C_3)$	minimize into	$(C_1 \cdot C_3)$
Cases	2 3	$(\sim C_1 \cdot C_2 \cdot \sim C_3)$ $(C_1 \cdot C_2 \cdot \sim C_3)$	minimize into	$(C_2 \cdot \sim C_3)$
Cases	3 4	$(C_1 \cdot C_2 \cdot \sim C_3)$ $(C_1 \cdot C_2 \cdot C_3)$	minimize into	$(C_1 \cdot C_2)$

The minimized statement is therefore

$$E = (C_1 \cdot C_3) + (C_2 \cdot \sim C_3) + (C_1 \cdot C_2)$$

These three prime implicants, however, cover the following primitive statements:

$(C_1 \cdot C_3)$	covers	$(C_1 \cdot \sim C_2 \cdot C_3)$ $(C_1 \cdot C_2 \cdot C_3)$	
$(C_2 \cdot \sim C_3)$	covers	$(\sim C_1 \cdot C_2 \cdot \sim C_3)$ $(C_1 \cdot C_2 \cdot \sim C_3)$	
$(C_1 \cdot C_2)$	covers	$(C_1 \cdot C_2 \cdot \sim C_3)$ $(C_1 \cdot C_2 \cdot C_3)$	(already covered by $[C_2 \cdot \sim C_3]$) (already covered by $[C_1 \cdot C_3]$)

Therefore, $(C_1 \cdot C_2)$ is a redundant prime implicant and can be eliminated

$$E = (C_1 \cdot C_3) + (C_2 \cdot \sim C_3)$$

meaning that E is caused either by the multiplication $(C_1 \cdot C_3)$ or by the multiplication $(C_2 \cdot \sim C_3)$. Both are sufficient but not necessary conditions for E (as each can be replaced by the other combination).

3. *Factorization*. The third device for simplifying causal statements is the factorization. More precisely, factorization helps in *clarifying* the structure of the data rather than simplifying it.

First, factorization helps highlighting *necessary conditions*. In the following causal statement:

$$E = (C_1 \cdot C_3) + (C_2 \cdot C_3)$$

C_3 is a necessary (but not sufficient, see Case 6) condition, whereas C_1 and C_2 are neither necessary (Cases 7 and 8) nor sufficient (Cases 4 and 5), as it appears in the table below. On the contrary, the two alternative (OR) combinations (AND) $C_1 \cdot C_3$ and $C_2 \cdot C_3$ are sufficient conditions for E.

Cases	C_1	C_2	C_3	$C_1 \cdot C_3$	$C_2 \cdot C_3$	E
1	1	1	1	1	1	1
2	1	1	1	1	1	1
3	1	1	1	1	1	1
4	1	0	0	0	0	0
5	0	1	0	0	0	0
6	0	0	1	0	0	0
7	0	1	1	0	1	1
8	1	0	1	1	0	1

Factoring the causal statement above is useful to show C_3 as a necessary condition:

$$E = C_3 \cdot (C_1 + C_2)$$

Second, factorization helps identifying *causally equivalent sufficient conditions*. In this example, C_1 and C_2 are equivalent in their combination with C_3 to produce two different combinations both of which are sufficient conditions for E. It does not matter (it is equivalent) with which condition C_3 combines. In both combinations it produces a sufficient condition.

Beyond Dichotomization:
Fuzzy Sets and the Use of Computer Programs

Because Boolean logic is a form of algebra in which all values are reduced to either "true" or "false," it has been crucial to the development of computer science based on 0/1 bit systems. Quite naturally, therefore, computer programs for the analysis of necessary and sufficient conditions with dichotomous data have developed in a number of fields, in particular in the fields of linguistics and text information retrieval (Zadeh, 1965), and search engines on the Internet. Initially based on dichotomous 0/1 systems, these retrieval methods have evolved to consider the frequency of terms in documents, allowing to weight information and transform systems to include *ordinal* or "*fuzzy*" *data* (Kraft, Bordogna, & Pasi, 1994; Meadow, 1992).

Social sciences have followed this evolution with Ragin's pioneering work on computer programs for Boolean analysis. The computer program for dichotomous data that was developed by Ragin and his collaborators— *Qualitative Comparative Analysis* (QCA)—was inspired by algorithms created by electrical engineers in the 1950s (Drass & Ragin, 1986, 1992; McDermott, 1985). Recently, a new software has been developed (Ragin, Drass, & Davey, 2003; Ragin & Giesel, 2003) to include fuzzy sets (*Fuzzy Set/Qualitative Comparative Analysis* or FS/QCA). Both programs are widely used and give rise to an increasing number of studies.[22]

The principles and rules for establishing sufficient and necessary conditions do not change when moving from dichotomous variables (0/1) to *ordinal* and *interval* (or ratio) variables. The aim of the comparative method is to identify sufficient and/or necessary conditions in the form of single attributes or, more typically, in the form of *configurations* (through specific combinations of attributes). Whether such configurations are constructed from 0/1 variables or from ordinal variables does not change the method of assessing if they are sufficient or necessary conditions for an outcome to occur.

Take the variable "state formation" operationalized as follows: "before 1815 (1)," "between 1815 and 1914 (2)," and "after World War I (3)." This variable can combine in different ways with a similar operationalization of "industrialization" "before 1870 (1)," "between 1870 and 1914 (2)," and "after World War I (3)." There are nine different configurations possible. With the methods above we can test which is either a necessary or sufficient condition (or both) for, say, high levels of national integration. Such combinations can also be done with interval or ratio variables: literacy rates among the adult population or urban density levels.

A recent way to move beyond dichotomization is to use *fuzzy-set approaches* (Mahoney, 2000, 2003; Ragin, 2000). Instead of being based on conventional "crisp" sets in which a case is either "in" or "out" (0/1) as in classical categorization, fuzzy sets allow membership in the interval between 0 and 1. For example, in a crisp set a family may be either "financially secure" or not. In a fuzzy set a family may be "almost" financially secure, say .85, that is, part of the set financially secure but not completely. *Fuzzy membership scores* are given to cases according to their degree of membership to the set. The United States does not fully belong to the set of "democracies" but almost (with a value of .80 according to Ragin, 2000, p. 176). This follows alternative ways of categorizing data such as family resemblance and radial categories.

Whereas in "variable-oriented" research categories are created *from* the values of the cases (a safe neighborhood is one in which the crime rate is, say, below 5% and a financially secure family is one with an income above, say, $40,000), in fuzzy sets "measurement" is carried out by attributing values to cases on the basis of the degree of belonging to a category or set. This is simply a different way of attributing *values to cases according to a given property* in which the knowledge of specific cases by the researcher plays a bigger role.

Finally, as with 0/1 data, compound statements are again formulated with the aid of *operators or connectives*—NOT, AND, and OR being the most important ones. With respect to conventional sets there are, however, some differences (Ragin, 2000, pp. 171–178). The two following subsections deal with the differences in the formulation of conditional statements. A discussion of how values are attributed to cases is not included.

Necessary and Sufficient Conditions

If C is a necessary condition for an outcome E, for all instances in which E is present, C must be present too. If "losing a war" is necessary for "social revolution," then there must be no social revolutions without "losing a war:" $P(\sim C \mid E) = 0$. However, we may find cases of "losing a war" where no social revolution has taken place ("losing a war" is not a sufficient condition). Thus, if all instances of $E = 1$ must also have $C = 1$ but there might be instances of $C = 1$ in which $E = 0$, then $E = 1$ is a subset of $C = 1$. Imagine 15 countries among which 10 have a PR electoral system and that, among these, 8 are MPS and 2 are TPS. All MPS have PR ($P(\sim C \mid E) = 0$) but not all PR lead to MPS (there are two "exceptions"). MPS = 1 (dependent variable) is a subset of PR = 1 (independent variable).

If the discrete values 0 and 1 are replaced by fuzzy values between the two extremes (degrees of proportionality of electoral systems and effective number of parties), this logic does not change. If a higher degree of proportionality is a necessary condition for a higher number of parties in a party system, then we must not find cases of higher number of parties with low levels of proportionality: $P(\sim C \mid E) = 0$. On the other hand, all instances of high number of parties must have also a high level of proportionality: $P(C \mid E) = 1$. However, we can have a high proportionality but few parties (since proportionality is necessary but not sufficient). As before, instances of many parties are a subset of instances with high proportionality.

The scattergram below depicts the theoretical distribution of values if C (proportionality) is a necessary condition for many parties (symbolized with •). When researchers find instances in which scores in the outcome are *less than* (*or equal to*) scores in the cause, then it is possible to conclude that we are in the presence of a necessary condition.

If C is a sufficient condition for an outcome E, for all instances in which C is present, E must be present too. If "losing a war" is sufficient for "social revolution," then there must be no "losing a war" without "social revolutions:" $P(C \mid \sim E) = 0$. However, we may find cases of social revolution that did not

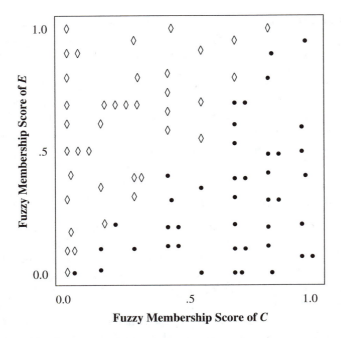

Fuzzy Membership Score of C

lose a war ("losing a war" is not a necessary condition: the same *E* can be caused by another factor such as "repressive regime"). Thus, if all instances of *C* = 1 must also have *E* = 1 but there might be instances of *E* = 1 in which *C* = 0, then *C* = 1 is a subset of *E* = 1. Imagine 15 countries among which 10 have MPS and that, among these, 8 are ethnically fragmented (FRAG) and 2 ethnically homogeneous. All FRAG are followed by MPS ($P(C \mid E) = 1$) but not all MPS need FRAG (there are two "exceptions"). FRAG = 1 (independent variable) is a subset of MPS = 1 (dependent variable).

Replacing discrete values with fuzzy values, if a higher degree of ethnic fragmentation is a sufficient condition for many parties, then we must not find cases of high ethnic diversity with few parties: $P(C \mid {\sim}E) = 0$. However, we can have a high number of parties without ethnic fragmentation (since fragmentation is not necessary and can be replaced by another factor such as PR). As before, instances of ethnic fragmentation are a subset of instances with many parties.

The theoretical distribution of values if *C* (ethnic fragmentation) is a sufficient condition for many parties is symbolized with ◊ in the scattergram above. When researchers find instances in which scores in the outcome are *more than* (*or equal to*) scores in the cause, then it is possible to conclude that we are in the presence of a sufficient condition.

Compound Statements

As above, the discussion is limited to the three main operators NOT, AND, OR.

1. *Negation: NOT*. In datasets with dichotomous variables the negation is the contrary of the value: the negation of 0 is 1 and vice versa. In fuzzy datasets the negation is given by the subtraction of the fuzzy membership score from 1:

Negation of fuzzy membership in set $A = 1 -$ [fuzzy membership score in set A]

For example, if the fuzzy membership score of Britain in the set "PR electoral systems" is .10, its negation (i.e., fuzzy membership in the set "non-PR systems") is .90:

$$\sim.10 = 1 - .10 = .90$$

In the table below the column $\sim C_1$ gives examples of negation scores for C_1.

2. *Conjunction: AND*. In datasets with dichotomous values the conjunction occurs when several factors must be present to produce an outcome $(C_1 \cdot C_2)$. Both factors must have a value of 1 to produce the outcome. In fuzzy data sets, cases may have different degrees of membership in the sets represented by C_1 and C_2 (see again the table below for an example). The fuzzy membership score of a case in the "conjunction set" of both factors is established by taking the *minimum* membership score.

Consider again a statement about the causes of MPS. In a dichotomous dataset, a hypothesis could be that the combination of PR and FRAG is a sufficient condition for producing MPS: PR · FRAG = MPS. If both are present, MPS is also present. To establish if a country is a "member" of the set of countries that have both PR and FRAG, we take the *minimum*.

Cases	PR C_1	FRAG C_2	Negation $\sim C_1$	Conjunction $C_1 \cdot C_2$	Disjunction $C_1 + C_2$
Britain	.10	.40	.90	.10	.40
Belgium	.95	.80	.05	.80	.95
Italy	.40	.20	.60	.20	.40

If a country, for example, the United States or India in the table below, score 0 on PR and 1 on ethnic fragmentation, the value of the compound statement PR · FRAG = 0, that is, the *smaller* value between PR = 0 and FRAG = 1. The same applies if we replace discrete values with fuzzy values. Suppose a country, say Britain in the table above, for which the fuzzy membership score on PR (the set of PR electoral systems) is .10 and on FRAG (the set of ethnically fragmented countries) is .40. In this case, the membership in the set of countries that are both proportional and fragmented is .10.

Cases	PR C_1	FRAG C_2	Negation $\sim C_1$	Conjunction $C_1 \cdot C_2$	Disjunction $C_1 + C_2$
United States	.00	1.00	1.00	.00	1.00
India	.00	1.00	1.00	.00	1.00

3. *Disjunction: OR.* The disjunction OR is the other most common operator used for compound statements. In conventional data sets, the disjunction occurs when one or another factor is present to produce an outcome $(C_1 + C_2)$. At least one of the two factors must have a value of 1 to produce the outcome, but not necessarily the two. In fuzzy data sets, cases may have different degrees of membership in the sets represented by C_1 and C_2. Contrary to the conjunction, the fuzzy membership score of a case in the "disjunction set" of several factors is established by taking the *maximum* membership score.

Taking again the same example, we may formulate the hypothesis that the compound statement PR or multimember constituencies (MM) is a necessary condition for MPS to occur, that is, that either PR or MM must be present but not necessarily both (PR + MM = MPS). A large constituency magnitude may have the same "proportionalizing" effects than PR even if the electoral formula is majoritarian. However, if both are absent the effect is not produced.

If a country, for example, Britain in the 19th century when most constituencies were multimember, score 0 on PR and 1 on magnitude, the value of the compound statement (PR + MM) is 1, that is, the *larger* value between PR = 0 and MM = 1. The same applies if we replace discrete values with fuzzy values. Suppose a country, say again Britain, for which the fuzzy membership score on PR (the set of proportional electoral systems) is .10 and on MM (the set of countries with multimember constituencies) is .70. In this case, the membership in the set of countries that have either PR or multimember constituencies is .70.

With these operators it is possible to formulate compound causal statements in terms of necessary and sufficient conditions as described in the previous subsection. These techniques—especially when powered by computerized software—allow sophisticated analyses well beyond the basic principles presented here.

CHAPTER 8. ASSESSMENT

Why, What, How to Compare

Why? We compare to control variation. First, only through comparison is it possible to establish differences and similarities between cases with respect to some attribute. Without comparison descriptive statements such as "densely populated" would be deprived of meaning. Whether we deal with nominal, ordinal, or interval measurements, it is only through comparison that types, orders, and quantities can be established. It is the comparison of the values of shared properties that allows us to identify similarities and differences, as well as change over time. Second, the comparative method allows us to control explanatory statements and systematically test against empirical evidence hypotheses concerning causal relationships between social phenomena in the form of "if . . . , then . . ." statements. Without comparison, whether we use methods based on Mill's methods and Boolean algebra, or statistical methods, the empirical test of the association between variables would not be possible. In this sense, there is no difference between case- and variable-oriented methods.

What? All is comparable. There are no logical limits to what is comparable. First, the comparative method applies to all types of units (such as territorial units, organizations, or individuals). Second, there are no limitations in space and time in the choice of cases. All cases are comparable as long as what is compared is not cases as such but cases' values of shared (common) attributes. This applies equally to Boolean techniques and statistics.

How? We compare through logic. First, taxonomical treatment allows us to define concepts able to "travel" and to make cases comparable. Second, classification rules allow us to isolate the relationship under investigation from the influence of other factors researchers wish to control for. Third, the use of logical methods developed from Mill's Methods of Agreement and Difference (or statistical methods) provide rigorous techniques to establish the empirical validity of statements about the association between phenomena. Fourth, the logical connectives AND/OR/NOT allow researchers to combine independent variables to form combinations and configurations of factors for each case. Fifth, logical methods allow the formulation of statements on causal connections in terms of necessary and/or sufficient conditions.

Strengths of the Comparative Method

Comparison has always been considered one of the most important intellectual devices to understand the world. Logical philosophers have put comparison at the center of their epistemologies for centuries. Comparison is at the heart of all methods, the experimental method (with comparisons between experimental and control groups), statistical methods (with comparisons, e.g., between groups in contingency tables or in analyses of variance), in the comparative method that developed in the last two decades in the wake of small-N studies and Boolean algebra (based on Mill's Methods of Agreement and Difference).

The first obvious strength of the comparative method is thus to make social sciences possible. In statistical analyses, comparison is associated with the introduction in the models of cross-country variation—in which properties (variables) at the country level are used as control or contextual variables. Comparison in this acceptation makes sense of variation that occurs cross-nationally or cross-temporally (if comparison is between time units) or cross-organizationally (if comparison is between agencies such as institutions, social associations, tribes, etc.). Techniques for analyzing rare phenomena and few cases through Boolean algebra have additional and different strengths.

From a *negative* perspective, the strength of Boolean techniques is to provide a solid and logically rigorous alternative when "unfavorable circumstances" make the use of other methods—namely, experimental and statistical methods—difficult or even impossible. Boolean comparative methods deal better than other methods with research questions for which problems of overdetermination are likely to arise (because of the "small N, many variables" problem) and with research questions involving qualitative properties and dichotomous variables, as well as higher risks of deterministic rather than probabilistic statements. These are "unfavorable circumstances" that should not imputed to Boolean methods themselves. Rather than seeing them as weak because they must deal with such circumstances, we should see the advantages of being able to deal with them when other methods fail, even though they do not provide measures of their conclusion as a statistical coefficient would do.

At the same time, however, from a *positive* perspective the comparative method based on logical algebra—can rely on a number of distinctive points of strength. The advantages of the comparative method are usually identified with

- its capacity to distinguish between *sufficient and necessary conditions*, that is, a logic of causation that goes beyond mere associations between phenomena;
- its capacity to take into account *multiple causation*; and
- its capacity to model independent factors as *combinations or configurations* of properties.

Converging Paths Between Methods

At several points in this volume, it has been argued that there are similarities among methods as far as the *fundamental principles* are concerned—such as the testing logic based on association and control. In addition, it is possible to detect an increasing convergence between statistical and comparative methods in the way each of them addresses *the distinctive features* of the other method. Currently, debates turn around the question of how statistics handles multiple causation, combinatorial explanations, categorical data and how the comparative method handles continuous data, and probabilistic explanations. In fact, it appears that the commonalities between the two approaches are more numerous than often thought.

Schematically, there are three main points of convergence.

Combinatorial Explanation

While it is often claimed that statistics does not include a combinatorial or configurational type of explanation, contingency tables, two-way ANOVA, and log-linear analysis show that this logic is present also in statistical techniques. Very similarly to Boolean algebra these techniques allow us to assess which type of combination of values of a number of dependent variables lead to an outcome (i.e., a specific value of the dependent variable). Multivariate contingency tables are perhaps the closest statistical "equivalent" to Boolean algebra in matters of combinatorial explanations.

Furthermore, interactions effects are, in multiple regression analysis, the equivalent of combinations. A change of value in the independent variable X_1 has an effect on the dependent variable Y only when another independent variable X_2 takes a given value. In this sense, interactive causal relationships do deal with a combinatorial type of causality (on interaction effects see Jaccard & Wan, 1996; Jaccard & Turrisi, 2003, in this same series).

Categorical Data Analysis

The same applies to categorical data analysis. Statistics offers a number of ways to deal with nominal/categorical measurement (even dichotomous) thus rejoining another specificity of Boolean algebra. *Contingency tables* are frequently used statistical techniques in comparative analyses as they allow one to deal with nominal/categorical data that—in broad historical comparisons especially—are often the main type of data.

Another technique that needs to be mentioned here is *regression with dummy variables* (see Hardy, 1993, in this series). If, for example, we have a nominal independent variable with, say, five religious groups, in regression analysis we would select one religion as the reference category and construct for each of the remaining religions a variable that as the value 1 when a case belongs to that religion and the value 0 if it belongs to any of the other religions. For each religion we have a dummy variable. The advantage of using regression analysis with dummy variables is that the output includes the precise effects of each of the groups of the independent variable (whose categories form the various dummies), whereas the output of, say, analysis of variance or contingency tables is limited to the general impact of the independent variable.

Finally, *log-linear analysis* is perhaps the most important technique used for categorical data analysis (see Ishii-Kuntz, 1994; Knoke & Burke, 1980, in this series). Special cases of log-linear analysis are logit models (or multinomial logistic regression) and probit models. All deal with binomial variables (the QASS series has produced a number of books, see e.g., Aldrich & Nelson, 1984; DeMaris, 1992; Kant Borooah, 2001; Liao, 1994; Menard, 2001; Pampel, 2000). Log-linear analysis can be considered a "regression-style" continuation of contingency tables techniques in which the number of variables can be higher (which would make a cross-tabulation unreadable and difficult to interpret). This technique allows one to decide which combination of factors (independent variables) has a stronger impact on the outcome of the dependent variable. In this sense, log-linear analysis is very close to the configurational and combinatorial nature of the comparative method. Furthermore, being a variation of regression analysis, log-linear analysis estimates the effect of each combination.

Summing up, therefore, if we consider statistical techniques such as multivariate contingency tables, two-way ANOVAs, log-linear analysis, and interactions effects, as well as considering the probabilistic and fuzzy-set evolution of Boolean algebra, it appears that the goals of the two approaches are not that different after all.

Probabilistic Relationships

Is Boolean comparative analysis deterministic? A number of authors have argued that the Methods of Agreement and Difference lead necessarily to deterministic results whereas statistical methods are probabilistic

86

(Goldthorpe, 1997a, 1997b, 2000, pp. 45–64; Lieberson, 1992, 1994, 1998). Here too, however, we see that differences are less striking than often argued.

- A causal proposition is said to be *deterministic* insofar as a given factor, when present, leads invariably to a specified outcome (when "X_1," then "Y"). One single case that runs against the hypothesized relationship leads to its rejection. The existence of one case in the opposite direction of that of the hypothesis would lead to conclude that "X_1" has no impact on "Y." Relationships are invariant and perfectly associated (correlations of ± 1.0).

- A causal proposition is said to be *probabilistic* insofar as a given factor, when present, increases the likelihood of a specified outcome (when "X_1," then the likelihood or frequency of "Y" increases). The existence of negative cases does not lead to the rejection of the relationship. Its rejection depends on the frequency (the researcher decides between the H_1 and the "null hypothesis"). Probabilistic propositions are based on associations that need not be perfect (correlations between ± 1.0).

Deterministic relationships do not occur in the social sciences. With such a "naive conception [one] would have not come very far" (Galtung, 1967, p. 505). Deterministic propositions are particularly unrealistic for the social sciences because of (1) *the nature of the data*—complex multivariate causal patterns; (2) *measurement errors*—the deviation of a set of data from the hypothesis is due to measurement errors rather than to the absence of the relationship; (3) *the impossibility to control for all factors*—researchers can attempt to control only for the factors they think, according to theory, may affect an outcome; and (4) *chance*—relationships by coincidence.

Moving from deterministic positions to forms of indeterminacy through the "probabilistic revolution" has therefore been an important advance in the social sciences (Krüger, Gigerenzer, & Morgan, 1987; Lieberson, 1985, pp. 94–97). In social research hypotheses are accepted or rejected on the basis of the *frequency* of positive and negative cases.

The idea that Mill's first two or three methods are deterministic is shared by researchers applying them to small numbers of cases. For Ragin "the [Method of Difference] is used to establish patterns of invariance. Imperfect (i.e., probabilistic) relationships are the province of statistical theory." And "they are designed to uncover patterns of invariance and constant association" (Ragin, 1987, pp. 39–40, 51), that is, invariant causal configurations that necessarily (rather than probably) combine to account for outcomes (Ragin & Zaret, 1983, pp. 743–744). For Skocpol (1984a) too, "[i]n contrast to the probabilistic techniques of statistical analysis . . . comparative historical analyses . . . attempt to identify invariant causal configurations that necessarily (rather than probably) combine to account for outcomes of interest" (p. 378).

However, the idea that the Boolean logic necessarily implies deterministic relationships between variables does not apply (and, in fact, was never intrinsic to its logic). Logical methods cannot be associated uniquely with deterministic propositions. In a *frequency distribution* perspective a factor can be accepted (corroborated) as sufficient or necessary condition not because there are no cases against the hypothesis, but because their frequency of "negative cases" is *low*. Comparative research can be based on frequency distributions in which the acceptance/rejection of a condition as necessary or sufficient is based not so much on its presence/absence in *all* instances but rather on its *degree* of presence/absence among the different cases compared. If we establish a level of acceptance of n (number of cases that we regard as sufficient to accept the hypothesis), the hypothesis is verified when the number of positive cases is $\leq n$ and reject if $\geq n$.

The level at which the acceptance or rejection of a cause can be established (n) is arbitrary. The *cut-off point* lies entirely in the hands of the researcher. With statistical methods, too, researchers arbitrarily decide if a relationship between independent and dependent variables is "strong" or "weak" (and, incidentally, a Pearson's $r = .30$ is often considered "strong" in the social sciences). The cut-off point depends obviously on the number of cases. Both Goldthorpe and Lieberson are right to argue that these methods are deterministic *not so much because of the logic as such* of the Methods of Agreement and Difference, but rather because of the *number of cases* (the small-N problem). Generally, it is correct to say that the smaller the N, the more one negative case is likely to lead to the rejection of the hypothesis. One negative case out of two leads to complete indeterminacy (50%) whereas one out of 10 is "less bad." Lijphart (1971) argues against the "fallacy of attaching too much significance to negative findings" but recognizes that "in the comparative analysis *of a small number of cases* even a single deviant finding tends to loom large" (p. 686, italics added).[23]

In this process deviant cases play an important role. They weaken but do not invalidate hypotheses. *Deviant case analysis* is one of the six types of case studies distinguished by Lijphart (1971, pp. 691–693). Case studies have an ambiguous status as "method" because they are not a generalizing activity. For many, therefore, case study analysis is not a method.[24]

However, deviant case analysis can be useful to reveal why cases are deviant and point to additional variables not considered in the original design. If used in this way, therefore, case studies can have a theoretical value. Deviant cases weaken the original hypothesis, but their study might suggest modified propositions that prove stronger.

CONCLUSION

Comparative methods developed in a period when social sciences were looking for a "general language," that is, theoretical and operational concepts that could be used without substantial, temporal, or spatial limitations. As mentioned, this process took place in conjunction with an objective expansion of the "N" through democratization processes in postcolonial areas and a subjective increase of interest, and thus data collections, in new countries. Such a move implied "replacing proper names with variables" (Przeworski & Teune, 1970), defining concepts able to "travel" (Sartori, 1970), and using "sets of universals" applicable to all social systems (Almond, 1966; Lasswell, 1968). In addition, because of the small number of cases for many research questions, a parsimonious use of variables was also invoked. This has led to "a strong argument against . . . 'configurative' or 'contextual' analysis" (Lijphart, 1971, p. 690) unable to lead to generalizing statements.

Early writings on the comparative method in the social sciences made strong arguments against "configurative" or "combinatorial" analyses in which a large number of potential explicative variables were listed (Braibanti, 1968, p. 49; Przeworski & Teune, 1970). This contrasts today with the tendency to develop complex, configurational, and combinatorial approaches. Thirty years later, a large part of the debates around methods in the social sciences focus on the opposite "reaction," namely a swing away from the "variable-oriented" approach in favor of a "case-oriented" and holistic approaches in which more properties are analyzed in "thicker" middle-range contexts. As Golthorpe notes, this represents a revival of holism against which Przeworski and Teune (1970) had directed their work stressing variables replacing "proper names." In addition, even if one concentrates on "whole" cases, one still refers to a number of their features or attributes. Comparison can take place only when one compares case's values of shared properties or attributes, that is, variables (Bartolini, 1993, p. 137; Goldthorpe, 2000). Reasoning in terms of "variables" is thus not specific to a "variable-oriented" approach, but rather is a common feature of both the variable- *and* case-oriented approaches.

Readers should be aware that this debate in the social sciences is not a recent one, but one that has been going on since the 1960s when "comparative approaches" have taken off in the various subdisciplines of the social sciences—mainly anthropology, sociology, and political science (comparative politics). Readers should, however, also be aware that, in spite of sometimes bitter debates, there are fundamental logical and methodological commonalities between the two approaches—one oriented toward large-N designs and statistical methods, one toward small-N designs and Boolean methods.

This volume has tried to stress these commonalities. Both approaches are ultimately variable oriented (even when the analysis of cases is a "thick" one). Both approaches can deal with configurational and combinatorial types of causality, as well as with the additive one. Both approaches are able to build models with different types of variables: discrete and continuous; categorical, ordinal, and interval. Both tend toward a probabilistic rather than deterministic assessment of causality. Each of these two approaches has distinctive strengths and weaknesses but the commonalities are probably more numerous than the differences. Probably, also, a more systematic and deeper "comparison," as it were, between the various methods would reveal even more, and even more fundamental, underlying commonalities.

To some extent, this book's aim was to show that many of comparison's principles are present in all methods for controlling variation in the social sciences—experimental, statistical variable-oriented approaches, and small-N case-oriented comparative ones—and thus provide the bases for progressing in the scientific endeavor beyond different approaches. Comparison should therefore be seen as *the fundamental underlying common logical principle in all methods*, making it possible to improve the accumulation of results and the collection/codification of data leading to more general results.

NOTES

1. The term qualitative is used here to indicate discrete, dichotomous, categorical, or nominal *levels of measurement*. The term does not indicate a *qualitative method*—such as ethnography, conversation analysis or content analysis of diaries, narratives, life stories, and discourses, or methods researching the visual and archives, or contextual analysis, participant observation, and self-observation (on these methods see Sage's series "Introducing Qualitative Methods"). In this sense, it is correct what many argue that the logic underpinning "qualitative comparative analysis" is, in fact, the same as the quantitative logic, that is, a positivist perspective based on the control of variation to test causality between independent and dependent variables.

2. The manipulation concerns both *experimental variables* (*operative* or *internal variables*, that is, those for which the researcher wants to test the impact) and *control variables* (*external variables*), which the researcher wants to "control for," that is, to exclude their influence from the relationship of interest.

3. The Joint Method of Agreement and Difference is also referred to as the "Indirect Method of Difference." The former label is used in this book in accordance with Mill's usage.

4. The comparative method is not the only one based on logic as sometimes it is argued. For this reason it is not possible to maintain that the distinctive feature of the comparative method is that it "is based on 'logical methods'" (Ragin, 1987, p. 15). Statistics, too, is based on logical principles.

5. Mill noted that "the concomitance itself must be proved by the Method of Difference" (Mill, 1875, p. 465).

6. The control of factors researchers wish to exclude from the relationship of interest between experimental independent and dependent variables concerns only factors that the researcher considers relevant based on previous knowledge, insights, and luck.

7. During this period an impressive number of works on the comparative method are imported from anthropology (Eggan, 1954; Radcliffe-Brown, 1951, 1958; Sjoberg, 1955).

8. Other QASS monographs deal extensively with all these methods. See, for example, Andersen (2007), Berry and Feldman (1985), Bray and Maxwell (1985), Breen (1996), Dunteman and Ho (2005), Fox (2000a, 2000b), and Lewis-Beck (1980, 1995).

9. Some authors prefer to speak of "few-N" rather than "small-N," with reference to the *number* of cases rather than their *size*. Bollen, Entwisle, and Alderson (1993, pp. 327–328) showed that already before the development of QCA and other software most comparative analyses were based on few cases.

10. Across-system diffusion should not be confused with (1) incrementalism or the change in a given variable building on previous changes in the same variable and

(2) global forces (the influence of variation over time of global conditions affecting all cases).

11. DF = $(N - V) - 1$, where N is the number of cases and V the number of independent (explanatory) variables. Thus, with two cases and one independent variable, DF = 0 and any claim about causation is worthless (Campbell, 1975).

12. King, Keohane, and Verba also suggest increasing the number of observations. As discussed above, however, this cannot always be done (see section Units of Analysis, point 4).

13. The term "category" is sometimes preferred to that of "concept" because it refers more directly to classification problems and to the boundaries of a concept (Collier and Mahon, 1993, p. 853).

14. The problem of equivalence leads to extreme criticisms from skeptic constructivist authors who question whether it is possible to have a science of comparative politics that formulates "cross-cultural, law-like causal generalizations" (MacIntyre, 1972, p. 9). This criticism bases on Mill's own warning about attempts to assume similarity in the social world in which similarities are superficial and misleading. Among the examples MacIntyre uses there is the concept of "pride" in Almond and Verba's (1963) *The Civic Culture*, which has a different meaning in Italy and in Great Britain, and that of "political party," which refers to different types of organizations in Africa and in the West.

15. In addition to these basic rules, classifications should also have a certain degree of stability, that is, they should not be changed too frequently especially when using longitudinal data, and should also be well balanced: (1) there should not be too many or too few categories and (2) there should be a balance of cases included in each category.

16. These alternative methods of categorization are based on set theory. A *third alternative* to classical categorization also based on set theory (or classification) are "fuzzy sets," which to some extent are based on, and formalize, other noncrisp classification methods. This is dealt with further down (see section Beyond Dichomomization: Fuzzy Sets and the Use of Computer Programs).

17. As De Meur and Berg-Schlosser (1994) note, the similarity of cases in MSSD concerns values of attributes of *independent* variables (whereas values of the dependent variable differ). For this reason they speak of Most Similar with Different Outcome designs (MS-DO). See below for a more detailed discussion.

18. The notation that uses C and E instead of p and q replaces simple statements with empirical properties or attributes.

19. This negative or eliminatory approach to confirmation is expressed more clearly in the *Method of Residues* (Fourth Canon), which reads as follows: "Subduct from any phenomenon such part as is known by previous inductions to be the effect of certain antecedents, and the residue of the phenomenon is the effect of the remaining antecedents" (Mill, 1875, p. 460). This is the most clearly eliminative method of all and applies to all methods. However, following Durkheim (*Les Règles de la Méthode Sociologique*) this method has no special utility in the social sciences where social phenomena are too complex to be able to eliminate the effect of all causes save one.

20. By *inclusive* disjunction what is meant is "whenever either one or both" components are true (the light is off because "either the switch is off or the bulb is burned out [or both]"). An *exclusive* disjunction is "either . . . or" but not both. This is expressed as $(C_1 + C_2) \cdot \sim(C_1 \cdot C_2)$.

21. The truth table for negations is the following:

C	$\sim C$
1	0
0	1

22. Software and manual are downloadable at www.u.arizona.edu/~cragin/fsQCA/ Other software programs exist such as TOSMANA (Tool for Small-N Analysis) developed by Lasse Cronqvist. See www.tosmana.org.

23. For this reason many authors prefer to use the terms corroboration rather than verification, and "weakening" rather than falsification or refutation.

24. As Zelditch (1971) noted, "case studies are of no use for explanatory purposes . . . For example, it could not be said from a study of the family in the United States that industrialization is a cause of the isolated nuclear family. Urbanization, the frontier, or a puritan heritage might equally well have caused it" (pp. 288–289).

GLOSSARY

Cause. Occurrence of an event supposed to bring about or produce the occurrence of another event.

Classification. Process and result of grouping cases by minimizing differences within each class and maximizing differences between classes, according to a dimension or property. Classes are mutually exclusive (no case should belong to more than one class) and jointly exhaustive (there should be a class for each case).

Comparative method. Method for testing against empirical evidence alternative hypotheses (and thereby either corroborate or reject them) about necessary and sufficient conditions for events to occur based on the association between configurations of values of different independent variables across cases, and the values of the dependent variable.

Conceptual stretching. Distortion occurring when a concept developed for one set of cases is extended to additional cases to which the features of the concept do not apply.

Configuration. Specific combination of the values of several properties (variables) for given cases.

Conjunction (Boolean multiplication). Logical connective producing a compound statement in which all components are true.

Control. Process through which the influence of some variables on the relationship between operational (independent and dependent) variables is either reduced or entirely eliminated.

Deduction. Type of inference based on a logical argument in which the truth of the premises guarantees the truth of a statement.

Deterministic relationship. Causal proposition in which a given circumstance, when present, leads invariably to a specified outcome ("if X, then always Y"). One single negative case leads to the rejection of the hypothesized relationship.

Dichotomization. Recodification of the values of multicategory nominal, ordinal, and continuous variables into binary values of 0/1.

Disjunction (Boolean addition). Logical connective producing a compound statement in which either (or all) components are true.

Equivalence. Feature of concepts and properties whose connotation is similar for all the cases compared.

Experimental method. Method based on the random assignment of subjects to treatment for testing against empirical evidence alternative hypotheses (and thereby either corroborate or reject them) about causal relationships based on the association between values of independent variables, which may be artificially modified, and the values of the dependent variable.

Extension (or denotation). Set (or class) of cases to which a concept refers.

Hypothesis. "If . . . , then . . ." statement about circumstances researchers suppose are relevant in explaining an event and subject to empirical falsification.

Induction. Type of inference based on a logical argument in which the support of empirical evidence guarantees the truth of a statement.

Intension (or connotation). Set of properties shared by cases to which a concept applies.

Ladder of abstraction. Also called "ladder of generality." Representation of the relation between intension and extension obeying a law of inverse variation. The larger the extension (and the smaller the intension), the higher the level of abstraction of a concept.

Matching. Method of control through the selection of cases whose values are constant.

MDSD (Most Different Systems Design). Research design in which the cases selected are characterized by different values on a large number of independent variables.

MSSD (Most Similar Systems Design). Research design in which the cases selected are characterized by similar values on a large number of independent variables.

Multicollinearity (historical). Association within a general process of change between the values of highly interlinked dependent and independent variables in which the units of observations are longitudinal time points or periods.

Multiple causation. Causal relationship in which the same effect is produced by different causes.

Necessary condition. Circumstance in whose absence a specified event cannot occur.

Negation. Logical connective producing a statement that reverses the truth value of any statement (simple or compound).

Negative case. Cases for which an event (most frequently the dependent variable) does not occur.

Overdetermination. Insufficient number of cases to test for all potentially relevant independent variables (low degree of freedom).

Probabilistic relationship. Causal statement in which a given circumstance, when present, increases the likelihood of a specified outcome. Few negative cases do not lead to the rejection of the hypothesized relationship.

Qualitative comparative analysis (QCA). Technique and computer program developed by Charles Ragin based on Mill's logic and Boolean algebra to test hypotheses about causal relationships between combinations of values of independent variables and the values of a dependent variable, in which the level of measurement is dichotomous. Fuzzy set/QCA extends the technique to multicategory variables.

Selection bias. (1) Distortion affecting the inference from sample to population arising from the nonrandom inclusion in the analysis of a number of cases chosen from a larger pool that are not representative of the population (external validity); (2) Overrepresentation of cases at one end or the other of the distribution of the dependent variable (internal validity).

Statistical method. Method for testing against empirical evidence alternative hypotheses (and thereby either corroborate or reject them) about causal relationships based on the association between values of independent variables across cases, and the values of the dependent variable.

Sufficient condition. Circumstance in whose presence a specified event always occurs.

Randomization. Method of control through the selection of cases whose values vary.

Taxonomy. Multidimensional classification in which classes are distinguished empirically.

Truth table. Chart displaying the possible combinations of truth values for a logical statement.

Typology. Multidimensional classification in which classes are distinguished conceptually.

REFERENCES

Aldrich, J. H., & Nelson, F. (1984). *Linear probability, logit, and probit models*. Quantitative Applications in the Social Sciences, No. 45. Beverly Hills, CA: Sage.

Almond, G. (1966). Political theory and political science. *American Political Science Review, 60,* 869–879.

Andersen, R. (2007). *Modern methods for robust regression*. Quantitative Applications in the Social Sciences, No. 152. Thousand Oaks, CA: Sage.

Armer, M. (1973). Methodological problems and possibilities in comparative research. In M. Armer & A. Grimshaw (Eds.), *Comparative social research: Methodological problems and strategies* (pp. 49–79). New York: Wiley.

Armer, M., & Grimshaw, A. (Eds.). (1973). *Comparative social research: Methodological problems and strategies*. New York: Wiley.

Bacon, F. (1620). *The new Organon (or true directions concerning the interpretation of nature)*. In J. Spedding, R. Ellis, & D. Heath (Trans.), *The Works* (Vol. 8). Boston: Taggard & Thompson (Translated work published 1863).

Bailey, K. (1982). *Methods of social research*. New York: Free Press.

Bailey, K. (1994). *Typologies and taxonomies: An introduction to classification techniques*. Quantitative Applications in the Social Sciences, No. 102. Thousand Oaks, CA: Sage.

Bartolini, S. (1993). On time and comparative research. *Journal of Theoretical Politics, 5,* 131–167.

Barton, A. (1955). The concept of property space in social research. In P. Lazarsfeld & M. Rosenberg (Eds.), *The language of social research: A reader in the methodology of social research* (pp. 40–53). New York: Free Press.

Benjamin, R. (1977). Strategy versus method in comparative research. *Comparative Political Studies, 9,* 475–483.

Berry, W., & Feldman, S. (1985). *Multiple regression in practice*. Quantitative Applications in the Social Sciences, No. 50. Beverly Hills, CA: Sage.

Blalock, H. (1961). *Causal inferences in nonexperimental research*. Chapel Hill: University of North Carolina Press.

Blalock, H., & Blalock, A. (Eds.). (1968). *Methodology in social research*. New York: McGraw-Hill.

Blaut, J. (1977). Two views of diffusion. *Annals of the Association of American Geographers, 67,* 343–349.

Bollen, K., Entwisle, B., & Alderson, A. (1993). Macrocomparative research methods. *Annual Review of Sociology, 19,* 321–351.

Bonnell, V. (1980). The uses of theory, concepts, and comparison in historical sociology. *Comparative Studies in Society and History, 22,* 156–173.

Brady, H., & Collier, D. (Eds.). (2004). *Rethinking social inquiry: Diverse tools, shared standards*. Lanham, MD: Rowman & Littlefield.

Braibanti, R. (1968). Comparative political analytics reconsidered. *Journal of Politics, 30,* 25–65.

Braumoeller, B., & Goertz, G. (2000). The methodology of necessary conditions. *American Journal of Political Science, 44,* 844–858.

98

Bray, J., & Maxwell, S. (1985). *Multivariate analysis of variance.* Quantitative Applications in the Social Sciences, No. 54. Beverly Hills, CA: Sage.

Breen, R. (1996). *Regression models: Censored, sample selected, or truncated models.* Quantitative Applications in the Social Sciences, No. 111. Thousand Oaks, CA: Sage.

Brown, S., & Melamed, L. (1990). *Experimental design and analysis.* Quantitative Applications in the Social Sciences, No. 74. Newbury Park, CA: Sage.

Burger, T. (1976). *Max Weber's theory of concept formation: History, laws, and ideal types.* Durham, NC: Duke University Press.

Campbell, D. (1975). "Degrees of freedom" and the case study. *Comparative Political Studies, 9,* 178–193.

Cohen, M., & Nagel, E. (1934). *An introduction to logic and scientific method.* London: Routledge & Kegan Paul.

Collier, D. (1991a). The comparative method: Two decades of change. In D. Rustow & K. Erickson (Eds.), *Comparative political dynamics: Global research perspectives* (pp. 7–31). New York: HarperCollins.

Collier, D. (1991b). New perspectives on the comparative method. In D. Rustow & K. Erickson (Eds.), *Comparative political dynamics: Global research perspectives* (pp. 32–53). New York: HarperCollins.

Collier, D. (1995). Translating quantitative methods for qualitative researchers: The case of selection bias. Review Symposium: The Qualitative-Quantitative Disputation. *American Political Science Review, 89,* 461–465.

Collier, D., & Mahon, J. (1993). Conceptual stretching revisited: Alternative views of categories in comparative analysis. *American Political Science Review, 64,* 1033–1053.

Collier, D., & Mahoney, J. (1996). Insight and pitfalls: Selection bias in qualitative research. *World Politics, 49,* 56–91.

Collier, D., & Messick, R. (1975). Prerequisites versus diffusion: Testing alternative explanations of social security adoption. *American Political Science Review, 69,* 1299–1315.

Cook, T., & Campbell, D. (1979). *Quasi-experimentation: Design and analysis issues for field settings.* Boston: Houghton Mifflin.

Copi, I. (1978). *Introduction to logic* (5th ed.). London: Macmillan.

DeMaris, A. (1992). *Logit modeling: Practical applications.* Quantitative Applications in the Social Sciences, No. 86. Newbury Park, CA: Sage.

De Meur, G., & Berg-Schlosser, D. (1994). Comparing political systems: Establishing similarities and dissimilarities. *European Journal of Political Research, 26,* 193–219.

Drass, K., & Ragin, C. (1986). *QCA: A microcomputer package for qualitative comparative analysis of social data.* Evanston, IL: Center for Urban Affairs and Policy Research, Northwestern University.

Drass, K., & Ragin, C. (1992). *Qualitative comparative analysis 3.0.* Evanston, IL: Institute for Policy Research, Northwestern University.

Dunteman, G., & Ho, M.-H. (2005). *An introduction to generalized linear models.* Quantitative Applications in the Social Sciences, No. 145. Thousand Oaks, CA: Sage.

Easthope, G. (1974). *A history of social research methods.* London: Longman.

Ebbinghaus, B. (2005). When less is more: Selection problems in large-N and small-N cross-national comparison. *International Sociology, 20,* 133–152.

Eggan, F. (1954). Social anthropology and the method of controlled comparison. *American Anthropologist, 56,* 743–763.

Evans-Pritchard, E. (1963). *The comparative method in social anthropology.* London: Athlone Press.

Fearon, J. (1991). Counterfactuals and hypotheses testing in political science. *World Politics, 43,* 169–195.

Fox, J. (2000a). *Multiple and generalized nonparametric regression.* Quantitative Applications in the Social Sciences, No. 131. Thousand Oaks, CA: Sage.

Fox, J. (2000b). *Nonparametric simple regression: Smoothing scatterplots.* Quantitative Applications in the Social Sciences, No. 130. Thousand Oaks, CA: Sage.

Frendreis, J. (1983). Explanation of variation and detection of covariation: The purpose and logic of comparative analysis. *Comparative Political Studies, 16,* 255–272.

Galtung, J. (1967). *Theory and methods of social research.* Oslo, Norway: Universitetsforlaget.

Geddes, B. (1990). How the cases you choose affect the answers you get: Selection bias in comparative politics. *Political Analysis, 2,* 131–152.

George, A. (1979). Case studies and theory development: The method of structured focused comparison. In P. Lauren (Ed.), *Diplomacy: New approaches in history, theory, and policy* (pp. 43–68). New York: Free Press.

Goertz, G., & Starr, H. (2003). *Necessary conditions: Theory, methodology, and applications.* Lanham, MD: Rowman & Littlefield.

Goldthorpe, J. (1991). The uses of history in sociology: Reflections on some recent tendencies. *British Journal of Sociology, 42,* 211–230.

Goldthorpe, J. (1994). The uses of history in sociology: A reply. *British Journal of Sociology, 45,* 55–77.

Goldthorpe, J. (1997a). Current issues in comparative macrosociology: A debate on methodological issues. *Comparative Social Research, 16,* 1–26.

Goldthorpe, J. (1997b). Current issues in comparative macrosociology: A response to the commentaries. *Comparative Social Research, 16,* 121–132.

Goldthorpe, J. (2000). *On sociology: Numbers, narratives, and the integration of research and theory.* Oxford, UK: Oxford University Press.

Grimshaw, A. (1973). Comparative sociology: In what ways different from other sociologies? In M. Armer & A. Grimshaw (Eds.), *Comparative social research: Methodological problems and strategies* (pp. 3–48). New York: Wiley.

Hardy, M. (1993). *Regression with dummy variables.* Quantitative Applications in the Social Sciences, No. 93. Newbury Park, CA: Sage.

Hempel, C. (1952). *Fundamentals of concept formation in empirical science.* Chicago: University of Chicago Press.

Hempel, C., & Oppenheim, P. (1948). Studies in the logic of explanation. *Philosophy of Science, 15,* 135–175.

Hoenigswald, H. (1963). On the history of the comparative method. *Anthropological Linguistics, 5,* 1–11.

Holt, R., & Richardson, J. (1970). Competing paradigms in comparative politics. In R. Holt & J. Turner (Eds.), *The methodology of comparative research* (pp. 21–71). New York: Free Press.

Holt, R., & Turner, J. (Eds.). (1970). *The methodology of comparative research.* New York: Free Press.

Ishii-Kuntz, M. (1994). *Ordinal log-linear models.* Quantitative Applications in the Social Sciences, No. 97. Thousand Oaks, CA: Sage.

Jaccard, J., & Turrisi, R. (2003). *Interaction effects in multiple regression* (2nd ed.). Quantitative Applications in the Social Sciences, No. 72. Thousand Oaks, CA: Sage.

Jaccard, J., & Wan, C. (1996). *LISREL approaches to interaction effects in multiple regression.* Quantitative Applications in the Social Sciences, No. 114. Thousand Oaks, CA: Sage.

Jackman, R. (1985). Cross-national statistical research and the study of comparative politics. *American Journal of Political Science, 29,* 161–182.

Kalleberg A. (1966). The logic of comparison: A methodological note on the comparative study of political systems. *World Politics, 19,* 69–82.

Kant Borooah, V. (2001). *Logit and probit: Ordered and multinomial models.* Quantitative Applications in the Social Sciences, No. 138. Thousand Oaks, CA: Sage.

King, G., Keohane, R., & Verba, S. (1994). *Designing social inquiry: Scientific inference in qualitative research.* Princeton, NJ: Princeton University Press.

King, G., Keohane, R., & Verba, S. (1995). The importance of research design in political science. *American Political Science Review, 89,* 475–481.

Klingman, D. (1980). Temporal and spatial diffusion in comparative analysis of social change. *American Political Science Review, 74,* 123–137.

Knoke, D., & Burke, P. (1980). *Log-linear models.* Quantitative Applications in the Social Sciences, No. 20. Beverly Hills, CA: Sage.

Kraft, D., Bordogna, G., & Pasi, G. (1994). An extended fuzzy linguistic approach to generalized Boolean information retrieval. *Information Sciences Applications, 2,* 119–134.

Krüger, L., Gigerenzer, G., & Morgan, M. S. (Eds.). (1987). *The probabilistic revolution: Vol. 2. Ideas in the sciences.* Cambridge: MIT Press.

Laslett, P., Runciman, W., & Skinner, Q. (Eds.). (1972). *Philosophy, politics, and society: Four series: A collection.* Oxford, UK: Blackwell.

Lasswell, H. (1968). The future of the comparative method. *Comparative Politics, 1,* 3–18.

Lauren, P. (Ed.). (1979). *Diplomacy: New approaches in history, theory, and policy.* New York: Free Press.

Lazarsfeld, P. (1937). Some remarks on typological procedures in social research. *Zeitschrift für Sozialforschung, 6,* 119–139.

Lazarsfeld, P. (1955). Interpretation of statistical relations as a research operation. In P. Lazarsfeld & M. Rosenberg (Eds.), *The language of social research: A reader in the methodology of social research* (pp. 115–125). New York: Free Press.

Lazarsfeld, P., & Barton, A. (1951). Qualitative measurement in the social sciences: Classification, typologies, and indices. In D. Lerner & H. Lasswell (Eds.). (1951). *The policy sciences: Recent development in scope and method* (pp. 231–250). Stanford, CA: Stanford University Press.

Lazarsfeld, P., & Rosenberg, M. (Eds.). (1955). *The language of social research: A reader in the methodology of social research.* New York: Free Press.

Lerner, D., & Lasswell, H. (Eds.). (1951). *The policy sciences: Recent development in scope and method.* Stanford, CA: Stanford University Press.

Levin, I. (1999). *Relating statistics and experimental design: An introduction.* Quantitative Applications in the Social Sciences, No. 125. Thousand Oaks, CA: Sage.

Lewis-Beck, M. (1980). *Applied regression: An introduction.* Quantitative Applications in the Social Sciences, No. 22. Beverly Hills, CA: Sage.

Lewis-Beck, M. (1995). *Data analysis: An introduction.* Quantitative Applications in the Social Sciences, No. 103. Thousand Oaks, CA: Sage.

Liao, T. (1994). *Interpreting probability models: Logit, probit, and other generalized linear models.* Quantitative Applications in the Social Sciences, No. 101. Thousand Oaks, CA: Sage.

Lieberson, S. (1985). *Making it count: The improvement of social research and theory.* Berkeley: University of California Press.

Lieberson, S. (1992). Small Ns and big conclusions: An examination of the reasoning in comparative studies based on a small number of cases. In C. Ragin & H. Becker (Eds.),

What is a case? Exploring the foundations of social inquiry (pp. 105–118). Cambridge, UK: Cambridge University Press.

Lieberson, S. (1994). More on the uneasy case for using Mill-type methods in small-N comparative studies. *Social Forces, 72,* 1225–1237.

Lieberson, S. (1998). Causal analysis and comparative research: What can we learn from studies based on a small number of cases? In H.-P. Blossfeld & G. Prein (Eds.), *Rational choice theory and large-scale data analysis* (pp. 129–145). Boulder, CO: Westview Press.

Lijphart, A. (1971). Comparative politics and comparative method. *American Political Science Review, 65,* 682–693.

Lijphart, A. (1975). The comparable-cases strategy in comparative research. *Comparative Political Studies, 8,* 158–177.

Lustick, I. (1996). History, historiography, and political science: Multiple historical records and the problem of selection bias. *American Political Science Review, 90,* 605–618.

MacIntyre, A. (1972). Is a science of comparative politics possible? In P. Laslett, W. Runciman, & Q. Skinner (Eds.), *Philosophy, politics, and society: Four series: A collection* (pp. 8–26). Oxford, UK: Blackwell.

Mackie, J. (1965). Causes and conditions. *American Philosophical Quarterly, 24,* 245–64.

Mackie, J. (1985). *Logic and knowledge: Selected papers.* Oxford, UK: Oxford University Press.

Mahoney, J. (2000). Strategies of causal inference in small-N analysis. *Sociological Methods and Research, 28,* 387–424.

Mahoney, J. (2003). Strategies of causal assessment in comparative historical analysis. In J. Mahoney & D. Rueschemeyer (Eds.), *Comparative historical analysis in the social sciences* (pp. 337–342). Cambridge, UK: Cambridge University Press.

Mahoney, J. (2004). Comparative-historical methodology. *Annual Review of Sociology, 30,* 81–101.

Mahoney, J., & Goertz, G. (2004). The possibility principle: Choosing negative cases in comparative research. *American Political Science Review, 98,* 653–669.

Mahoney, J., & Rueschemeyer, D. (Eds.). (2003). *Comparative historical analysis in the social sciences.* Cambridge, UK: Cambridge University Press.

McDermott, R. (1985). *Computer-aided logic design.* Indianapolis, IN: Howard W. Sams.

Meadow, C. (1992). *Text information retrieval systems.* San Diego, CA: San Diego Academic Press.

Meckstroth, T. (1975). "Most different systems" and "Most similar systems": A study in the logic of comparative inquiry. *Comparative Political Studies, 8,* 133–157.

Menard, S. (2001). *Applied logistic regression analysis* (2nd ed.). Quantitative Applications in the Social Sciences, No. 106. Thousand Oaks, CA: Sage.

Mill, J. S. (1843/1875). *A system of logic: Ratiocinative and inductive: Being a connected view of the principles of evidence and the methods of scientific investigation, Vol. 1* (9th ed.). London: Longmans, Green, Reader, & Dyer.

Moore, F. (Ed.). (1963). *Readings in cross-cultural methodology.* New Haven, CT: HRAF Press.

Moul, W. (1974). On getting something for nothing: A note on causal models of political development. *Comparative Political Studies, 7,* 139–164.

Nagel, E. (Ed.). (1950). *John Stuart Mill's philosophy of scientific method.* New York: Hafner.

Nagel, E. (1961). *The structure of science.* New York: Harcourt, Brace, & World.

Nagel, E., Suppes, P., & Tarski, A. (Eds.). (1963). *Logic, methodology, and philosophy of science.* Stanford, CA: Stanford University Press.

Naroll, R. (1961). Two solutions to Galton's problem. *Philosophy of Science, 28,* 15–39.

Naroll, R. (1964). A fifth solution to Galton's problem. *American Anthropologist, 66,* 863–867.

Naroll, R. (1965). Galton's problem: The logic of cross-cultural analysis. *Social Research, 32,* 428–451.

Naroll, R. (1968). Some thoughts on comparative method in cultural anthropology. In H. Blalock & A. Blalock (Eds.), *Methodology in social research* (pp. 236–277). New York: McGraw-Hill.

Naroll, R., & D'Andrade, R. (1963). Two further solutions to Galton's problem. *American Anthropologist, 65,* 1053–1067.

Pampel, F. (2000). *Logistic regression: A primer.* Quantitative Applications in the Social Sciences, No. 132. Thousand Oaks, CA: Sage.

Parsons, T. (1949). *The structure of social action.* New York: Free Press.

Pennings, P., Keman, H., & Kleinnijenhuis, J. (2007). *Doing research in political science: An introduction to comparative methods and statistics* (2nd ed.). London: Sage.

Peters, G. (1998). *Comparative politics: Theory and methods.* London: Macmillan.

Popper, K. (1959). *The logic of scientific discovery.* New York: Basic Books.

Popper, K. (1989). *Conjectures and refutations: The growth of scientific knowledge.* London: Routledge.

Pryor, F. (1976). The diffusion possibility method: A more general and simpler solution to Galton's problem. *American Ethnologist, 3,* 731–749.

Przeworski, A., & Teune, H. (1970). *The logic of comparative social inquiry.* New York: Wiley Interscience.

Radcliffe-Brown, A. (1951). The comparative method in social anthropology. *Journal of the Royal Anthropological Institute, 81,* 15–22.

Radcliffe-Brown, A. (1958). *Method in social anthropology.* Chicago: University of Chicago Press.

Ragin, C. (1987). *The comparative method: Moving beyond qualitative and quantitative strategies.* Berkeley: University of California Press.

Ragin, C. (1997). Turning the tables: How case-oriented research challenges variable-oriented research. *Comparative Social Research, 16,* 27–42.

Ragin, C. (2000). *Fuzzy-set social science.* Chicago: The University of Chicago Press.

Ragin, C., & Becker, H. (Eds.). (1992). *What is a case? Exploring the foundations of social inquiry.* Cambridge, UK: Cambridge University Press.

Ragin, C., & Giesel, H. (2003). *User's guide to fuzzy-set/qualitative comparative analysis 1.1.* Tucson: Department of Sociology, University of Arizona.

Ragin, C., & Zaret, D. (1983). Theory and method in comparative research: Two strategies. *Social Forces, 61,* 731–754.

Ragin, C., Drass, K. A., & Davey, S. (2003). *Fuzzy-set/qualitative comparative analysis 1.1.* Tucson: Department of Sociology, University of Arizona.

Ross, M., & Homer, E. (1976). Galton's problem in cross-national research. *World Politics, 29,* 1–28.

Roth, C., Jr. (2004). *Fundamentals of logic design* (5th ed.). Belmont, CA: Thomson, Brooks, & Cole.

Rustow, D., & Erickson, K. (Eds.). (1991). *Comparative political dynamics: Global research perspectives.* New York: HarperCollins.

Sartori, G. (1970). Concept misformation in comparative politics. *American Political Science Review, 65,* 1033–1053.

Sartori, G. (1984a). Guidelines for concept analysis. In G. Sartori (Ed.), *Social science concepts: A systematic analysis* (pp. 15–85). Beverly Hills, CA: Sage.

Sartori, G. (Ed.). (1984b). *Social science concepts: A systematic analysis.* Beverly Hills, CA: Sage.

Sartori, G. (1991). Comparing and miscomparing. *Journal of Theoretical Politics, 3,* 243–257.

Sigelman, L. (1977). How to succeed in political science by being very trying: A methodological sampler. *Political Science and Politics, 10,* 302–304.

Sjoberg, G. (1955). The comparative method in the social sciences. *Philosophy of Science, 22,* 106–117.

Skocpol, T. (1979). *States and social revolutions: A comparative analysis of France, Russia, and China.* Cambridge, UK: Cambridge University Press.

Skocpol, T. (1984a). Emerging agendas and recurrent strategies in historical sociology. In T. Skocpol (Ed.), *Visions and methods in historical sociology* (pp. 356–391). Cambridge, UK: Cambridge University Press.

Skocpol, T. (Ed.). (1984b). *Visions and methods in historical sociology.* Cambridge, UK: Cambridge University Press.

Skocpol, T., & Somers, M. (1980). The uses of comparative history in macrosocial inquiry. *Comparative Studies in Society and History, 22,* 174–197.

Smelser, N. (1966). Notes on the methodology of comparative analysis of economic activity. In *Transactions of the Sixth World Congress of Sociology* (pp. 101–117). Evian: International Social Science Association.

Smelser, N. (1973). The methodology of comparative analysis. In D. Warwick & S. Osherson (Eds.), *Comparative research methods* (pp. 42–86). Englewood Cliffs, NJ: Prentice Hall.

Smelser, N. (1976). *Comparative methods in the social sciences.* Englewood Cliffs, NJ: Prentice Hall.

Stinchcombe, A. (1978). *Theoretical methods in social history.* New York: Academic Press.

Strauss, D., & Orans, M. (1975). Mighty shifts: A critical appraisal of solutions to Galton's problem and a partial solution. *Current Anthropology, 16,* 573–594.

Swanson, G. (1971). Frameworks for comparative research: Structural anthropology and the theory of action. In I. Vallier (Ed.), *Comparative methods in sociology: Essays on trends and applications* (pp. 141–202). Berkeley: University of California Press.

Sztompka, P. (1988). Conceptual frameworks in comparative inquiry: Divergent or convergent? *International Sociology, 3,* 207–218.

Teune, H., & Ostrowski, K. (1973). Political systems as residual variables: Explaining differences within systems. *Comparative Political Studies, 6,* 3–21.

Thrupp, S. (1970). Diachronic methods in comparative politics. In R. Holt & J. Turner (Eds.), *The methodology of comparative research* (pp. 343–358). New York: Free Press.

Tilly, C. (1975a). Reflections on the history of European state making. In C. Tilly (Ed.), *National states in Western Europe* (pp. 3–83). Princeton, NJ: Princeton University Press.

Tilly, C. (Ed.). (1975b). *National states in Western Europe.* Princeton, NJ: Princeton University Press.

Tilly, C. (1984). *Big structures, large processes, huge comparisons.* New York: Russel Sage Foundation.

Tylor, E. (1889). On a method for investigating the development of institutions applied to the laws of marriage and descent. Reprinted in F. Moore (Ed.), *Readings in cross-cultural methodology* (pp. 245–272). New Haven, CT: HRAF Press.

Vallier, I. (Ed.). (1971). *Comparative methods in sociology: Essays on trends and applications.* Berkeley: University of California Press.

van Deth, J. (Ed.). (1998). *Comparative politics: The problem of equivalence.* London: Routledge.

104

von Wright, G. (1951). *A treatise on induction and probability*. London: Routledge & Keagan Paul.

Warwick, D., & Osherson, S. (Eds.). (1973). *Comparative research methods*. Englewood Cliffs, NJ: Prentice Hall.

Wellhofer, S. (1989). The comparative method and the study of development, diffusion, and social change. *Comparative Political Studies, 22*, 315–342.

Zadeh, L. (1965). Fuzzy sets. *Information Control, 8*, 338–353.

Zelditch, M., Jr. (1971). Intelligible comparisons. In I. Vallier (Ed.), *Comparative methods in sociology: Essays on trends and applications* (pp. 267–307). Berkeley: University of California Press.

INDEX

Analogy, 42
Analysis of variance, 13
Analytical construct, 35
Anthropology, 8, 38–39
Attributes:
  comparative method, 28–29
  comparison, 1–2
  defined, 1

Bacon, F., 42
Biased causality, 19
Biased inference, 19
Biology, 6–7
Boolean algebra, 4, 14
Boolean distance, 47, 49
Boolean operators:
  combinatorial causation, 68–69
  combining connectives, 69–71
  compound statements, 79–81
  conjunction (AND) (multiplication),
    65, 66–67, 68–75, 79–80, 94
  data simplification, 71–75
  disjunction (OR) (addition), 65–66,
    67–68, 69–75, 79, 80–81,
    93n20, 94
  fuzzy-set analysis, 77, 79–81
  multiple causation, 67–68
  multivariate analysis, 64–75
  necessary condition, 68–69
  negation (NOT), 66, 79, 80, 93n21
  sufficient and necessary
    condition, 70–71
  sufficient condition, 67–68
  sufficient nor necessary
    condition, 69–70
  truth table, 65, 66, 68, 69, 70, 71,
    72, 73, 74, 75

Case-oriented research:
  deviant case analysis, 87–88, 93n24
  dummy variables, 15

  nominal variables, 15
  small-scale comparative
    studies, 12, 14, 15
  social sciences, 89–90
  taxonomical treatment, 29–30
Case selection:
  control strategies, 37–38
  cross-sectional unit, 16, 21–23
  diachronic comparative
    research, 17–19
  functional unit, 16
  individual unit, 16
  necessary condition, 59–61
  sufficient condition, 57, 58
  temporal unit, 17
  units of analysis, 16–18
Case selection bias:
  biased causality, 19
  biased inference, 19
  cross-sectional case, 20, 21–23
  defined, 96
  diffusion, 21–23
  external validity, 19
  "Galton's problem," 21–23, 91n10
  generalization bias, 19
  historical contingency, 20–21
  historical sources, 24–25
  internal validity, 19
  limited variety/diversity, 21
  MDSD (Most Different Systems
    Design), 22–23
  Method of Agreement, 20
  negative case, 20, 23–24
  research design, 20
  self-selection, 20–21
  specification bias, 19
  temporal unit, 20
Categorical variables, 25–26
Causation:
  conditional statement,
    41–42, 43–45, 52

106